# THE THEORY OF ECONOMIC EXTERNALITIES

Institut Universitaire de Hautes Etudes Internationales
Collection d'Economie Internationale

2

International Economics Series

# THE THEORY OF ECONOMIC EXTERNALITIES

## The Control of Environmental Pollution and Similar Social Costs

JAMES E. MEADE

1973
A. W. SIJTHOFF - LEIDEN
Institut Universitaire de Hautes Etudes Internationales
GENÈVE

# Preface

*This short book is based on three lectures given at the Graduate Institute of International Studies in Geneva in December 1972. I would like to thank the Director of the Institute for the invitation to lecture. The preservation of the environment from excessive pollution is a matter which already raises many international issues and which will raise many more as the years pass. Pollution of the environment is an outstanding example of external diseconomies; and in choosing the theory of economic externalities as the subject for my lectures in Geneva my hope was that, although I was not dealing specifically with the international aspects of these problems, yet a discussion of the basic character of externalities would prove a useful introduction to those who intended to specialise on the international applications of the theory.*

*My indebtedness to the many scholars who have developed this subject will be obvious to any economist who glances at the following pages. Indeed it is invidious to pick out names from so large a company of writers from whom I have derived the ideas in this book. But I must mention: the way in which Chapter III is based on the work of such men as Professors Coase, Buchanan and Tullock; the way in which I have learned from Professors Beckerman and Lerner about the control of externalities through taxation which I discuss in Chapter IV; and, finally, the way in which the last pages of Chapter IV and the whole of Appendix B are based upon some important ideas of Dr. Starrett, as developed by Professors Baumol and Bradford.*

*J. E. M.*

*Christ's College, Cambridge.*
*December 1972.*

# Contents

# I. The Definition of Externalities

At first sight the distinction between an 'internal' effect and an 'external' effect in the analysis of economic activities seems straightforward. I hire a carpenter to mend my table. The service which I get from having my table mended and the benefit which he receives from the wage which I pay him are all internal to the transaction which takes place between us. But suppose that his hammering disturbs my neighbour's enjoyment of the snooze which he was taking in his garden. This effect is external to the transaction between the carpenter and myself, who together took the decision to mend the table in my house ; the noise has not annoyed the carpenter or myself but someone who was outside or external to our decision and took no part in reaching it.

It seems reasonable, therefore, to adopt the following definition :

> "An external economy (diseconomy) is an event which confers an appreciable benefit (inflicts an appreciable damage) on some person or persons who were not fully consenting parties in reaching the decision or decisions which led directly or indirectly to the event in question."

At first sight this definition seems straightforward and innocuous ; and I shall in fact adopt it. But there lie hidden behind it a great number of questions, which I shall now try to answer. In fact the problem of deciding exactly where one wishes to draw the line between an internality and an externality in economic analysis is not at all straightforward ; and the definition which I have adopted casts the net very widely.

The first point to notice is that an economic decision may be taken by one decision-maker or jointly by a number of decision-makers. If I decide to mend my table myself, there is a single decision-maker ; if I hire a carpenter to do it, there are two decision-makers reaching a joint

15

decision, since I must decide to hire him and he must decide to be hired. In either case, if the hammering disturbs my neighbour, there is an externality, since in neither case was he a consenting party to the decision. All sales and purchases are joint decisions ; and both the buyer and the seller are consenting parties to (i.e. internal to) the transaction. The same is, I suggest, true of gifts, if the recipient of the gift is free to decide whether to accept or not ; both the recipient and the donor are internal to the single decision.

But what about taxes ? Who are the decision-makers in a governmental public-finance decision ? Suppose that I am subjected to a higher rate of tax in order to finance a higher rate of pension for the impoverished old-age pensioner. Am I external or internal to this decision ? I may well approve of the decision ; and in any case if I live in a parliamentary democracy in which there is a right to free speech I shall have had the opportunity both to take part in choosing those ministers and legislators who have imposed the tax and also to persuade them to adopt or not to adopt this policy. But I may have voted for those who are opposed to this policy and I may have been very vocal in trying to persuade those in authority of the unwisdom of their policy. Of course, even in this case I may well be a consenting party to the institutional process (e.g. parliamentary democracy) by which the decision is reached, but I am hardly a fully consenting party to this particular decision. If this is so, then my definition of an externality would put the effects of the tax on me in the category of an externality.

I think that it is appropriate to include in the analysis of externalities all the theory of public goods and of public taxes and subsidies. I shall give reasons for this view in Chapter II when I come to discuss the classification of the reasons which lead to externalities. My definition is intended to make this clear by referring to those who are external to the decision in question as those who are not *fully* consenting parties in reaching the decision.

But if the events caused by those in governmental authority are to be treated as externalities in so far as they affect the governed, what about the decisions of other persons in authority ? The child who creeps unwillingly to school because the authority of his parents bids him to do so may in fact be receiving what will turn out in the future to have been a precious gift ; but by no stretch of the imagination can he be said to have been a fully consenting party in reaching the decision to be sent to school. It is an externality for him.

16

Similarly, in the case of a slave economy where the master simply uses his authority to direct the life and work of the slave, the events in his life are externalities ; the slave is not a fully consenting party in reaching the decisions which give rise to them.

The case of the child in his minority and of the slave in his servitude present no problem of interpretation. If my definition is accepted, the commands which they have to obey are externalities.

A difficult problem of interpretation arises, however, in the case of an employer exercising authority over an employee. An employer directs an employee to turn from job A to job B ; the employer is acting within the terms of the contract with the employee, but the employee would rather continue at A than turn to B. Is the employee a fully cnnsenting party in the employer's decision ? The facts of the case may be clear and it is, of course, only a matter of how we choose to use words whether we call this event in the employee's life an externality or not. But I think that most of us would not find it useful to treat this decision as an externality ; and the question thus arises whether with my definition we can exclude it from the category of externalities.

I think that we can legitimately do so. Yesterday the joint decision of employer and employee was that the employee should work at A ; it was a free decision of the employee since he was not a slave and could always have given notice to his employer. Today the joint decision of employer and employee is that the employee should work at B ; and this also is a free decision on both sides. The whole thing is internal to the contract between employer and employee.

Let us leave it at that for the moment, though I do not really believe that it is quite as simple as that and I shall want to return to this case in due course. But let us consider first a more stringent use of an employer's authority. Clearly when an employer engages a worker, this must be treated as a joint decision. The employer must agree to hire the worker and the worker must agree to be hired by this employer. But suppose now that a long established worker is unwillingly dismissed from his job—perhaps very reluctantly—by his employer because the market for the firm's product has slumped. If we are to be at all realistic, this is not a joint decision, it is a decision taken solely by the employer and is one in which the employee is not a fully consenting party.

We need not rush to the conclusion that the worker's dismissal is an external diseconomy, even if we agree that the worker cannot be treated as having been a fully consenting party to the decision. In terms of my

17

definition it is an external diseconomy only if "the event inflicts an appreciable damage" on the dismissed employee. Suppose that there were a perfect market for the labour of the dismissed worker. Without incurring any additional costs of movement or training he could obtain at the same market wage another job of equal attractiveness. His dismissal would "inflict no damage" on him. There would be no external diseconomy.

This analytical point is of basic importance in thinking about economic externalities. In a world of perfect markets in which there were no real effects (such as noise) which were not the subject of transactions in perfect markets, there would be no externalities. This would be so even if all decisions were taken by single decision-makers. In order that there should be perfectly competitive markets all decision-makers would have to operate on a small scale ; otherwise a single decision-maker could influence market prices. No decision-maker could himself make more than a marginal change in any market ; and since every relevant event would be the subject of a market transaction and since prices would equal marginal costs in every market, any indirect marginal change resulting from a single decision-maker's decision could not cause any appreciable net benefit or damage to anyone.

I suspect strongly that it is because we are so steeped in analysis which starts with the assumption of perfect competition that whenever we think of externalities we think of things like noise or smoke which are real effects which can lie totally outside an otherwise complete set of perfect markets. But I suggest that we must be careful to decide how we treat internalities and externalities in cases in which it is not a question of perfect markets on the one hand and no market at all on the other ; but in which there are imperfect and monopolistic markets, as well as the operations of governments to which I have already alluded.

Let me tell a story involving the straightforward classical theory of monopoly. For some reason or another which we need not specify some group of citizens who had previously not bought any of a monopolist's product now decide to spend some part of their income on it. The monopolist producer reacts to this increased demand either (i) by producing and selling the same quantity of his product but at a higher price than before or (ii) increasing his output and selling a larger quantity at the same price as before.

Let us start with case (i) — Let us consider the quantity of the monopolist's product which the previous purchasers continue to purchase after the rise in price ; in respect of this quantity there is a redistribution of income from the previous purchasers to the monopolist, since a larger sum of money is paid for the same quantity of the product. These previous customers are fully consenting parties to their purchases from the monopolist both at the lower price before the change and at the higher price after the change. But the monopolist's bargaining power has been improved as a result of the decision on the part of the new customers who have caused an increase in the demand for his product. The previous customers of the monopolist were in no sense fully consenting parties to this decision of their fellow citizens to enter the market for the mono-polist's product. The damage done to these previous customers and the corresponding benefit to the monopolist due to the increased bargaining power of the monopolist is indirectly due to a decision in which neither they nor the monopolist played any part. This is an external economy to the monopolist and an exactly offsetting external diseconomy to his previous customers due to a decision of the new customers, a decision in which neither the monopolist nor his previous customers played any part.

Where, as in the present case, an external effect takes the form of a redistribution of income due to a price effect we may call it a 'distribu-tional externality'.

Let us turn to case (ii) where the monopolist sells more at the same price when the demand for his product is increased as a result of the decision of the new customers to enter the market. There will now be a 'real-income externality', if without hurting anyone else this confers an appreciable benefit on the monopolist who was not a party to the decision of the new customers to enter the market. And this may well be the result.

Solely to simplify the exposition, suppose that the increased spending on the monopolist's product may be treated as a small marginal addition to the monopolist's sales and that this monopolist's market is the only example in the whole economy of an exception to a perfectly competitive system which covers all goods and services. Then this change does appreciably benefit the monopolist without helping or hurting anyone else. Any additional workers employed by the monopolist to produce the additional output, coming as they do from a perfectly competitive labour market, are indifferent at the margin between working for him or for anyone else. The purchasers of the product are at the margin indif-ferent between spending this money on the monopolist's product or on any other product at the ruling prices. There is a marginal divergence between social cost and social value in the monopolist's market but nowhere else ; and anything which causes a marginal increase in that output will increase total real income. The monopolist gains his monopoly margin on the extra sales and no-one else is worse off.

I have dealt with this sort of analysis at length in terms of 'second-best' policies in Part I of my *Trade and Welfare* and in my *Theory of Customs Unions*. The point is a simple one. Where there are marginal divergencies between values and costs due to taxes, monopolistic elements, or to 'externalities' more narrowly defined, a change in outputs will cause an increase in total real income if the sum of the changes in quantities each multiplied by its marginal divergence is greater than zero. Any decision which leads indirectly to such a change may, I suggest, be said to carry with it a 'real-income external economy'. On consideration it seems to me unhelpful to draw a hard-and-fast line between those cases in which there is literally no market (as for a factory's smoke) and those cases in which there is a very imperfect market for something (as in the case of our monopolist's product). A change in quantities which in either case confers a benefit or damage which is not fully requited in the market should, I suggest, be treated as an external economy or diseconomy.

If we accept this way of treating externalities, the problem of the redundant worker who is unwillingly dismissed falls into place. If his dismissal is seriously unwilling, it means that to that extent the labour market is imperfect. He cannot get another job elsewhere which is equally attractive in pay and other conditions. If his 'opportunity wage' elsewhere is much lower than in his existing job, then there is a divergence in his existing job between his 'earnings' and his 'cost' to society. So long as the value of his marginal product in the existing job remains higher than it would be in his next most productive use, his dismissal does cause a loss of real income to the community. There is a real income externality in the decision of the employer to dismiss him. [1]

Let us return for a moment to the definition of distributional externalities. If we accept our definition, we must, I think, be prepared to concede that, while no 'real-income externality' could occur if there were perfectly competitive markets covering all goods and services, yet 'distri-

---

[1] From the point of view of the maximisation of the community's output, valued at current prices, it might be better to reduce his wage rate until it was no longer greater than his marginal value to the employer in his existing job. But this may well be ruled out on institutional grounds, which, in turn, may be based on distributional considerations. But this should not interfere with our definition of an external diseconomy as following his dismissal.

butional externalities' might well occur even in a complete system of perfect competition.

Let me make my point by giving a simple example. There is an island which produces nothing but sugar ; the land is all owned by one class of sugar barons ; and the sugar is produced on this land by one class of workers called cane-cutters. There is perfect competition ; the sugar barons receive the marginal product of their land and the cane cutters the marginal product of their labour. A further group of men, expelled cruelly and unjustly from their existing homeland, decide to come to the island and work as cane-cutters ; more labour is employed per acre of land ; the marginal product of the land and so the rent of land rises, while the marginal product of labour and so the wage rate falls. Every factor receives the value of its marginal product both before and after the immigrants' decision to add themselves to the labour force.

The decision of the immigrants has, however, affected the distribution between cane-cutters and sugar barons of the intra-marginal output of sugar which was already being produced by the existing cane-cutters before the newcomers' decision to immigrate into the island. Their decision has indirectly caused the existing workers to receive a smaller price for their labour although they are conferring the same real benefit in the form of sugar output as before and it has caused the landlords for the contribution of their land to this previous sugar output to receive a higher price than before. The immigrants by their decision to immigrate, in which in my story neither the sugar barons nor the existing cane-cutters played any part, have caused two offsetting external effects—an external diseconomy to the existing cane-cutters and an external economy to the sugar barons. With my definitions this must be admitted as a straightforward 'distributional externality'.

I will close this discussion of my definition of externalities by referring to a very troublesome matter. We of this generation have inherited a great stock of capital goods and of other intangible forms of wealth (such as technical knowledge) which has been accumulated as the result of the efforts and sacrifices of our forebears. This has certainly "conferred upon us an appreciable benefit" through decisions in which, since we were not even born at the time, "we were not fully consenting parties". Clearly our forebears have taken decisions which have resulted in external economies which we have enjoyed.

But let us consider this at the micro level, as it were. I decide to save in order to leave something to my children. It is a gift from me to them. They could refuse to take it. They are "fully consenting parties" to this joint decision on my part to give, and on their part to receive, a given amount. If the present accumulation of real capital for the present generation has occurred through a series of micro joint decisions in each of which both benefactor and beneficiary were fully consenting parties, how does the externality arise at the macro level?

We must, I think, be very careful to avoid one tempting way of resolving this apparent paradox. Assuming that no one will refuse a gift, one might well argue that my bequest to my child is not a joint decision but a decision taken by me in reaching which my child was not a party. Certainly a gift is a very one-sided decision. My child might well prefer that I should have been more abstemious and have left £1,000,000 instead of the £1 which I am leaving to him. Just as when he was a minor and I commanded him to go to school (i.e. to do something he did not want to do), so when I am making my will and I decide exactly how much (if any) he should receive of something which he would like to receive, it might be defined as my decision and not a joint decision. In that case, in terms of my definition of an externality, both his going to school when a minor and receiving £1 in my will is an external effect for him.

There is danger in adopting this solution of our problem. The receipt of a gift is an extreme case of a joint decision over which one party (the giver) has much influence and the other (the recipient) has little influence, being able merely to refuse the gift or to take what is offerred to him. But there is in fact a whole continuous spectrum of distribution of power of influence in joint decisions. Again one must beware of habits of thought which are appropriate only for perfectly competitive markets. In such a market there is no room for play on the part of buyer or seller ; the buyer will not pay more than the ruling market price at which he can purchase and the seller will not take less than the ruling market price at which he can sell. But in an imperfect market where there is, for example, an element of bilateral monopoly this is not so. The seller will sell for anything over £1 ; the buyer will buy for anything less than £10. If the buyer is a stronger character and stands out successfully for a price of £1, is this a joint decision or is it a decision in reaching which the seller is not a fully consenting partner? If we are not careful, we shall open the floodgates and be saying that there is a larger or smaller degree of externality in every transaction, and that it is only in perfect competition that this degree becomes zero. I think we must say that a person is a fully consenting party to any decision over which he did not exercise a power of veto which he might have exercised. It is for this sort of reason that at an earlier stage I argued that when a worker was ordered to turn from job A to job B, the shift should be regarded as the result of a joint decision, even though the worker would have preferred to stay at job A. He could have vetoed the change by leaving the employment.

If we take this line, my bequest to my child is a joint decision of myself and my child. One cannot explain the externality involved in the capital equipment received by one generation from previous generations by defining my bequest as a decision to which my child was not a party. There is, however, another line of attack on the micro level. My ability to leave capital to my child will depend not only on my own abstemiousness during my lifetime, but also on the amount which I have previously inherited from my parents. Their bequest to me was a decision to which I was a party, but my child was not a party to that early decision. This earlier decision has indirectly led to a change in my 'bargaining power' in my present joint decision with my child as to my bequest to him. Thus the additional amount which he receives because my parents were generous to me in their wills is a decision in which my son has played no part, but which has indirectly led to an event which is to his advantage. We need at least three generations to explain the externality of the passage of capital from one generation to another.

So much for the tiresome and formal problem of defining economic externalities.

# II. The Conditions
# Leading to Real-Income Externalities

I turn now to a discussion of what are the technological and institutional conditions which may give rise to real-income externalities. This I shall do by enumerating six different sets of conditions which may have this effect.

### (1) *The Shared-Variable Set of Conditions*

Let me start with what is probably the most basic type of externality, which I will call externalities due to a shared variable. Indeed this is so basic a type that externalities are sometimes narrowly defined simply as cases in which the same particular variable enters into the utility function or the cost function of more than one independent economic decision-maker. It is not, of course, simply that both A and B enjoy the consumption of the same class of goods—for example, that each gets enjoyment from the possession of his own country cottage ; the case arises when the particular country cottage which A builds and enjoys gives pleasure or pain to B by improving or spoiling B's view.

The particular variable which is shared may be common to A's and B's utility function, as in the case just given. Or it may be shared in A's and B's cost function, as in the case where the particular factory which A builds to reduce his costs blocks the light from B's factory and thus raises B's bill for electric lighting. Or it may be shared in A's cost function and in B's utility function, as in the case where the cheap method of production adopted by A causes a smoke nuisance which affects the enjoyment by B of his nearby home. Moreover the shared variable may be to the advantage of both A and B, to the disadvantage of both A and B, or to the advantage of one and to the disadvantage of the other.

Where there is a particular tie of this kind between A's and B's utilities and costs there cannot be an effective market for the variable in question.  In order that there should be such a market for any particular good or service it is necessary that the seller should be able to play off one buyer against another and/or that the buyer should be able to play off one seller against another.

Take a very simple case of bilateral monopoly.  Suppose that A and B are geographically close to each other and that we are considering the sale by A to B of something which has very high costs of transport.  A can sell only to B and B can buy only from A.  The particular item which passes from A to B, if it does so pass, must appear both in A's cost function and in B's utility function.  If for this reason A is unable to say to B —"If you won't offer me a higher price, I will withdraw my supply from you and sell to C"—and if at the same B is unable to say to A—"If you won't let me have it at a lower price, I will withdraw my custom and purchase it from D"—there can be no market in the product.

This straightforward case of bilateral monopoly can be treated as a case of a shared variable.  If A and B do manage to strike a bargain, then the particular good which passes from A to B enters into A's cost function and into B's utility function, and it could not enter into any cost function other than A's or any utility function other than B's.  But, on the other hand, the transaction is due to a joint decision of A and of B ; A cannot force the good on an unwilling B, and B cannot obtain the good from an unwilling A.  Moreover, the transaction, if it does take place, does not affect the interest of any third party.  It does not fall within our definition of an externality as given at the beginning of Chapter I.

It is when a shared variable can, as it were, be imposed upon one agent by a unilateral decision of the other agent that the shared-variable case falls within our definition of an externality.  I shall at a later stage discuss at some length a parable of apple-farmers and bee-keepers in which the bees feed on the nectar in the apple blossom and in which an externality arises because apple-farmer A would find it prohibitively costly to arrange to charge bee-keeper B for the nectar sucked by B's bees out of A's apple blossom.  Suppose, however, that there were no such costs involved ; the nectar taken from any tree by any bee can be cost-lessly measured and a money payment can be costlessly collected by an apple-farmer from a bee-keeper.  But suppose that the geographical lie of the land was such that apple-farmer A's apple blossom could be reached only by bee-keeper B's bees.  There can now be no market because A cannot offer his nectar to anyone but B, and B cannot acquire his nectar from anyone but A.  But in this case A can take a unilateral

28

decision. If A decides to produce apple blossom, B gains ; and if A decides not to produce apple blossom, B loses ; and that is that. There is a straightforward external economy in A's action.

This type of technological or geographical tie between the action of some particular economic agent and the effect on some particular victim or beneficiary or more generally on some group of particular victims or beneficiaries can take many forms. All the cases of what are often regarded as the most typical externalities—smoke nuisance, noise, river pollution etc.—fall into this big category. Indeed externalities are often defined as the phenomena which fall into this category of the shared variable and we may perhaps refer to them as 'externalities narrowly defined'.

The two concepts of externalities—as narrowly defined in this category and as widely defined in Chapter I above are, however, both rather elusive. Somewhat paradoxically it is not in fact even obvious that all the phenomena covered by the 'narrow' definition are necessarily included in those covered by the 'wider' definition.

Let me illustrate this by another simple case. There are two neighbours, A and B, and the question arises whether there should be a fence between their gardens. A wants the fence to give him shade from the sun ; B dislikes the fence because it cuts off his view of a beautiful countryside.

The actual outcome in a case like this may depend upon who has legal right to decide the issue. If A has the right to build the fence or to maintain the fence if it is already built, then the fence will exist unless B is prepared to pay A a sufficient sum to persuade him not to build the fence. If B has the right to veto the building of a fence or to insist on its removal if it already exists, then the fence will not stand unless A is prepared to pay B a sufficient sum to persuade him to put up with the fence. Or conceivably the law might be that everything remains as it is unless both A and B agree upon a change. But this does not basically alter the analysis. If the fence exists, then it will continue to exist unless B will pay A sufficient to agree to its removal ; if the fence does not exist, it will not be built unless A will pay a sufficient compensation to B. This is merely to say that the legal rights of A and B are determined by whatever happens to be the existing situation of the fence ; the analysis of what happens once the legal rights are settled remains unaltered.

But whoever has the legal right to decide, this case is clearly a case of an 'externality as narrowly defined' ; the same particular fence clearly enters into both A's and B's utility function. But it can be questioned whether it does in fact fall within the 'wider' definition given in Chapter I. Let us illustrate from the case in which A has the legal right to decide. The case for treating it as an externality in terms of the wider definition is clear. A can reach a decision, namely to build the fence if it is not there or to maintain it if it is already there ; and this is a decision to which B is not a party, but which imposes an appreciable damage on B. But it might be argued that this is too formal a way of treating such a case. In effect the outcome is a joint decision of A and B, but one which is taken in a very imperfect market. Thus A has decided to build the fence because of the simultaneous decision of B not to pay him sufficient compensation to persuade him not to build the fence. If B had been willing to pay a sufficient compensation, there would have been a joint agreement that the fence should not be built.

As in so many cases, it is a question of convenience how one treats borderline cases. I myself would prefer to treat this case as an externality within the wider definition, because it is only the simplest case of a much larger category of cases ; and the more one moves into this larger territory of cases, the less natural it becomes to treat them as joint decisions taken in imperfect markets rather than as decisions taken by a single economic agent but with effects on outsiders who had no direct part in reaching the decision.

Consider a case where the particular action of decision-maker A affects the utilities of a number of other particular citizens B, C, D, etc. The familiar example of a smoke nuisance is a case in point. The factory owned by A belches smoke which affects the particular housewives B, C, D, etc. who live in the neighbourhood. It is technically impossible to guide the smoke so that it is concentrated on Mrs. B's and Mrs. C's laundry and does not affect that of Mrs. D. Suppose that A has the legal right to produce the smoke ; it is impossible for Mrs. D to pay A to keep the smoke from her laundry and to direct it on to Mrs. B and C instead. It needs a joint decision of Mrs. B, C, and D to club together to make a combined payment to A to persuade him to go in for some form of expensive smoke abatement.

Or if Mrs. B, C, and D have the right to clean air, Mr. A cannot pay Mrs. B and Mrs. C to take his smoke, leaving Mrs. D unsullied. He must persuade all of them simultaneously to take the smoke.

Such a situation involves two very well known difficulties.

First, there are the purely administrative costs of arranging a joint

30

decision to which all the parties—A, B, C, D, etc.—must simultaneously agree. They must all get together and hammer out a joint agreement by which B, C, D agree on individual subscriptions to a common fund which is in total sufficient to persuade A to abate his smoke ; or, if the housewives have the legal right to clean air, B, C, D, etc, must agree on a set of individual compensations which is sufficient to compensate each of them for the smoke nuisance and which add up to a sum which A is prepared to pay for the right to belch forth his smoke.

Reaching such joint decisions will not only involve organisational difficulties and administrative costs ; it raises also all the problems connected with bargaining. Suppose A has the right to belch smoke and suppose that the sum of the maxima that each of B, C, D would pay to get rid of the smoke is greater than the sum necessary to meet A's costs of smoke abatement. It will not necessarily be easy to reach a joint decision. Mrs. B pretends only to be willing to pay a small amount, because she has a shrewd idea that Mrs. C and D are really ready together to pay enough to get rid of the smoke. But Mrs. D and Mrs. C may play the same bargaining game. Mr. A in turn may pretend to need more in total than is really necessary to meet his smoke abatement costs because he thinks that Mrs. B, C, and D are together really prepared to contribute more.

Similar bargaining problems arise if Mrs. B, C, and D start with the right to clean air. Mr. A will be tempted to offer less in total than the real value to him of the right to emit smoke ; and Mrs. B, C, and D will each be tempted to overstate the amount they need to allow the smoke to be emitted.

Suppose A has the legal right to emit the smoke and suppose the smoke is emitted. It is conceptually possible to describe this as a joint decision of A, B, C, and D to have the smoke on the grounds that it implies that B, C, and D made a tacit joint decision not to offer A enough to induce him to enter into a joint decision not to emit the smoke. But when the number of persons becomes at all large, the administrative and bargaining problems of reaching a unanimous joint decision become so overwhelming that the realistic possibility of an actual joint decision must be ruled out. The case must be treated as a decision by the single agent A to do something which damages B, C, and D, who had no part in the decision.

The limiting case of this is the public good. The expenditure by the government on defence may affect the utility of every citizen—increasing the utility of some by increasing their sense of security, but decreasing the utility of the pacifists. It is conceivable that, if one could get over the administrative costs and the bargaining difficulties of the operation, one could call a meeting of all citizens in the Albert Hall in which the voluntary subscriptions of those who wanted the defense less compensating payments to the pacifists were sufficient to cover the defense bill. There would then be a unanimous joint decision. But this is clearly an absurd way of looking at the problem. The decision to spend the money on defense and to raise the revenue by a particular set of taxes is in fact a decision of the government to which the individual citizens are not directly parties but which affects appreciably the welfare of every citizen. Public goods are clear examples of externalities.

Even the above unconvincing parable of the unanimous joint decision reached on defense at the Albert Hall meeting disappears when we treat public decisions to affect the distribution of income and wealth. I have already argued this case in Chapter I. When rich Mr. A is taxed unwillingly to subsidise poor Mr. B, by no stretch of the imagination can this be treated as a joint decision of A and B. We must all live in an egalitarian or all live in an inegalitarian society. One cannot have the rich man living in an inegalitarian society and the poor man in an egalitarian society. This is only the most obvious case of those general social conditions which we must all experience together, which affect everyone's utility function. They are in fact forms of 'public goods',—social variables which must be shared by every member of the community.

Before closing our discussion of the shared variable there are three notes which may be added.

First, the particular persons who may share the variable in their utility or costs functions with the economic decision maker may be unknown at the time at which the decision is taken. Consider the use of DDT by a farmer the value of whose crop is at once increased by the use of this pesticide. The actual identity of the person who years later will be harmed by the DDT after it has moved up the food chain into the mother's milk of some particular infant not yet born may be completely unknown. Nevertheless there is a variable shared between that particular farmer's cost function and that particular infant's utility function in the future. On both the narrow and the wide definition this is an externality.

Second, externalities of the shared-variable variety may be caused by indivisibilities and increasing returns to scale. Of course indivisibilities and increasing returns may give rise to monopolistic conditions which may lead to a marginal divergence between prices and costs and so to an externality in the way already described in Chapter I. But there is another form of connection between indivisibilities and externalities, which in these cases fall into the shared-variable class.

Consider a telephone network. If A instals a telephone, it increases the scope of the network which the existing subscribers B, C, D can use. They can now communicate with A as well as with each other. Normally this will be a decision of A which is to the advantage of B, C, and D because of the economies of scale in a network of this kind ; but it is, of course, possible that if A is a frightful bore, the possibility that he can now tackle B, C, and D at home over the telephone as well as directly in the club may reduce the value of the network to B, C, and D. But in either case all share a common variable in their utility functions, namely the size and scope of the total telephone network.

A different type of this same phenomenon can arise from the more familiar cases of increasing returns to scale, Because of economies of large-scale production there will be room in the market for only a limited number of products from which consumers may make their choices. There may, for example, be room in the market for only two car models although there are, say, six models—A, B, C, D, E, F,—all of which are equally easy to produce. Some consumers might prefer models C and D to have been put on the market, whereas in fact it is models A and B which have been selected for production. This is clearly analogous to a 'public good'. All consumers who are interested in cars at all have to share the same range of choice between available models. The actual car which I buy is a 'private' good ; it enters my utility function and not yours. But the range of cars from which we can choose is a 'public' good which we must share in common.

This combination of the 'private' and the 'public' aspect of a good is very widespread. To take only one more example, consider a domestic piped water supply which is metered and charged at its marginal cost to the individual domestic consumers. The amount of water which I consume is a private good ; if I drink an extra pint of the stuff, it will not affect you. But the quality of the water is a public good. The water authority might be able to supply a very high quality, soft water at a high price or a low quality, hard water at a low price. You and I must both share the same quality and in this aspect water is a public good.

Finally, it may be noted that these shared variables cover such moral qualities as envy and sympathy. Jones has received a higher income than I and is able to afford a coloured television set while I cannot.  If this makes me green with envy or if it makes me rejoice to see my neighbours happy, then Jones's consumption of a coloured television set has entered my utility function.  This must be defined as an externality of the shared-variable class, though whether or not one should do anything about it is another matter altogether.

## (2) *The Ill-defined-Ownership Set of Conditions*

The second set of conditions which gives rise to a real-income externality is where there is some scarce resource such that the more you use the less there is for me, but where the resource has not been ascribed to the ownership of any specified economic agent.  Let us call this the 'ill-defined-ownership' set of conditions.  This is a familiar case and is probably the most straightforward of all from my present taxonomic point of view.  I shall merely repeat two very familiar examples of it.

There is a pool of oil lying under an area of land, different parts of which are owned by many different owners.  Every landowner sinks a well on his own land.  The more oil B C D E and F have pumped out of their wells, the lower the level in the pool and the more expensive it will be for A to pump from his well later.  A will, therefore, pump as quickly as he can.  For similar reasons, B will pump as quickly as he can ; and so on, all over the series of wells.  As a result everyone pumps away as quick as he can, much quicker than would be economic if there were a well-defined single owner of the oil, because each wants to get the oil before the other.

A second example is over fishing in the oceans.  If whales are not all that abundant, the more whales everyone else catches the less there are for me to catch.  This case differs in a very important respect from the previous case of a single pool of oil pumped by many independent operators.  The oil once used cannot be replaced.  The whales if they are allowed to remain in sufficient numbers will reproduce themselves and will provide a continuing source of supply, whereas if they are sufficiently over caught they will become extinct.  But the basic trouble is the same. If each breeding group of whales were owned by a particular owner, there could be a perfectly competitive market for whales and they would be exploited with proper regard for the maintenance of the supply ; but as long as they are owned by no one, each individual whaler (in the absence of some other regulation) will operate with no regard for the future supply,

34

since if he limits his catch it will simply mean that some other whaler will expand his catch.

### (3) *The Market-Organisation-Cost Set of Conditions*

Let me turn to the third set of conditions which may lead to real income externalities. Until recently economists have been very apt to neglect the administrative and other costs involved in organising and running a market. In recent years it has become clear that in dealing with monetary theory and with the closely connected problem of planning to meet an uncertain future, a basic element in the analysis is the fact that organising and using all the possible markets for all the possible contingent goods and services must be ruled out on grounds of cost. The question as to what limited number out of the infinite possible number of forward markets and of insurance markets it will pay to organise has become a central feature of monetary theory and of the theory of planning for the future. I suggest that a similar set of questions should now become a central feature of the theory of external economies. Let us call this the 'market-organisation-cost' set of conditions leading to real-income externalities.

I will enumerate in due course a large number of more or less realistic instances to illustrate my thesis. But I will start with what is, I fear, an artificial, unreal example simply because I am familiar with it and familiarity has in this case bred affection rather than contempt. Let us suppose then that in a particular area there is a very large number of independent competing apple-farmers and that in the same region there is a very large number of independent competing bee-keepers. Stretch your imaginations to the full and suppose that every bee-hive is approximately the same distance from every apple tree. I know little of the technology of apple orchards or bee keeping ; but I assume that the more nectar your bee sucks from a particular piece of apple blossom, the less nectar there is for my bee to suck.

The stage is now set for a very simple straightforward competitive market. Each apple-farmer sets a ticket collector with a pair of scales at each apple tree and each bee-keeper sets a beeman at each hive with some ingenious electronic, chemical, or biological device—or failing that with the simple mechanical device of a cage or net—for guiding or carrying that set of bees to any particular apple tree. Each beeman takes his bees to suck at a particular tree, choosing that tree where the price of nectar is lowest—of course, with due regard to the quality of the nectar. Each ticket collector weighs each bee before and after sucking to discover the amount of nectar taken and charges a price for the nectar. There will result a perfect market for nectar. Each apple-farmer in planning his operations will have just the correct incentive to produce a good supply of his bye-product nectar, as well as of his main crop apples. Each bee-keeper will have just the right incentive to restrain his demands on nectar instead of treating it as a free good and neglecting the fact that he is taking it from his neighbours' bees.

But you have, I suspect, already observed the snag. The market would be so expensive to organise relatively to the revenue to be gained by the apple-farmers that it would never come into existence ; and I am pretty confident that in this case it should never come into existence. The result will be that the apple-farmers when they decide to produce apples confer an external economy on the bee-keepers ; and the individual bee-keeper by extending his hives confers an external diseconomy on the neighbouring bee-keepers, since he deprives them of a part of the supply of nectar.

One result of a complete absence of any market for nectar is to make the situation resemble that of the pool of oil or the school of whales. It may be that if it ever got a law court there would be no doubt about the ownership of the nectar in the apple blossom on my apple tree ; it belongs to me. But the fact that in no conceivable circumstances would I ever incur the expense of asserting my ownership means that, so far as the bee-keepers are concerned, it is as if the ownership of the nectar were not determined. The case jumps for practical purposes, as it were, from the 'market-organisation-cost' set of conditions causing externalities to the 'ill-defined-ownership' set ; and I regret to have to remind you that earlier on slightly different assumptions this example was found in the 'shared-variable' class. I note these awkward facts because the boundaries between our various taxonomic classes of externalities are, I fear, somewhat elastic.

One of the reasons why I cited this far-fetched example of the supply of nectar was that I wanted to isolate the 'market-organisation-cost' as a reason for externalities from the other possible reasons. But in the real world many of the different reasons for externalities may exist at the same time ; and in all of the more realistic examples of 'market-organisation-cost' which I will now enumerate there are in fact other elements of externality as well.

36

As a general rule the postal service in a country charges different prices for products according to their weight, but not according to the distance to be covered or the remoteness of the final destination, although the cost of delivering the packet is increased by the distance to be covered and the remoteness of the destination.  This does lead to some external effects.  When I post a letter which is going to travel an exceptionally long distance to an exceptionally remote place, I impose an extra cost on the system for which I do not pay.  But the cost of administering a more elaborate charging system might outweigh any improvement in the use of resources due to encouraging letters over short distances to easy destinations relatively to letters over long distances to remote destinations.

Whether or not a more elaborate pricing system should be introduced into any market in order to make charges approximate more closely to the marginal cost of providing the service depends in the first place upon the elasticities with which the quantity of the service demanded by the consumers and supplied by the producers will respond to the price charged to the consumer or paid to the supplier.  At one extreme, if there were no consequential change in quantity there could be no real income effect ; at the other extreme if a small change in price would cause a large change in quantity (if for example a small charge paid by bee-keepers to apple-farmers would induce a large change in the supply of nectar), then *pro tanto* there is a stronger case for trying to improve the accuracy of the pricing system.

But whether or not it will in fact be worthwhile to carry out any improvement in the accuracy of the price mechanism will depend also upon a second factor, namely the cost of administration of the price mechanism relatively to the other operational costs of the activity.

In some cases forms of charging which depend upon sophisticated metering devices have recently become cheaper relatively to other expenses, as a result of advance in electronics and in computing machinery. We may take charges for local telephone calls as a case in which externalities have been reduced because more sophisticated metering arrangements have made a more accurate use of the price mechanism possible. Whereas a fixed charge used to be made for each call, however long the call might last, now it is relatively easy to make the charge depend upon the length of the call and the time of day at which it is made.  Both of these factors affect the true social cost of the call, since the number of other persons who are impeded from use of the system which will carry only a certain volume of communication at a time will depend both upon the length of time and the time of day at which I use the system. Elaborate book keeping has in this case become cheaper and more practicable as a result of recent technological advances in metering and computing.

In other cases recent economic changes have made it preferable to shift to simpler pricing principles and to face any loss due to the less accurate reflexion of social costs in prices charged. In some cities now a single flat-rate charge is made for entering a public transport bus no matter how short or long the distance to be travelled. Contrast this with the system of charging according to the distance travelled. The former system saves in administration of the pricing system, since there need be no control other than some simple mechanism to ensure that each passenger pays the fixed charge on entering the bus. But the cost of transport is in fact greater, the greater the distance travelled ; and it is in principle desirable to charge so as to discourage long as contrasted with short journeys. The increase in economic efficiency so achieved may be worthwhile if the bus routes are long with many intermediate stops and if the cost of selling individual passenger tickets is low relatively to the other costs per mile of running the bus. But charging individual bus tickets is labour-intensive in so far as it involves having a bus conductor as well as a driver on the bus. A rise in the wage of labour relatively to the price of the petrol consumed per mile covered by the bus may, therefore, tip the balance in favour of abandoning a charge according to the distance travelled and adopting a fixed charge for entering the bus.

But the social costs of travel does not depend only upon the distance travelled but also upon such factors as the time of day and the direction of travel. Consider an underground network in a big city. The social cost of travel per passenger-mile is higher if the line is congested so that more passengers mean either more trains or more discomfort of those packed into the carriages or longer queues and more delays for those who are waiting to travel. To avoid externalities anyone who wishes to make a journey in such circumstances should pay an extra charge to cover the additional costs and hardships which his presence imposes on the other passengers ; and this means that journeys at times of day and in directions which are likely to be in high demand (for example, going into the city in the morning at a time that work starts or returning to the suburbs in the evening when work stops) should be charged at a higher price.

This would involve charges adjusted according to distance, time of day, and direction. Professor Vickrey once suggested an ingenious scheme. You put a high-priced coin into a ticket machine when you enter the underground network and receive a ticket which records the place and time of your entry ; when you leave the system you put this ticket with this information into another machine which, controlled by a computer, charges you the appropriate fee for a journey of that distance, in that direction, and that time of day by returning to you an appropriate amount of change out of the high-priced coin which you have paid for the original ticket. Perhaps modern metering and computing devices would make possible more refined pricing systems of this kind.

The use of the roads by cars causing noise, stench, danger to life and limb, and congestion is another case in point. The amount of social cost involved depends upon the place (e.g. country lane or city road), the time of day, the speed, and the direction of the journey. It is a relatively easy administrative matter to charge cars by taxation according to the horse power of the engine or the amount of petrol consumed, But this does nothing to give special discouragement to those journeys which cause most hardship to others. The question arises whether by more sophisticated metering devices it would be possible, and if so whether it would be worth the additional administrative costs, to charge according to the place and time at which a journey was made. The range of sophistication of conceivable devices is almost unlimited from, at the one extreme, an electronic meter carried in every car which can be operated to clock up charges according to place, direction, speed, time of day, etc. to, at the other extreme, a simple toll charge for entering certain particularly congested areas such as big city centres.

Charges for the domestic supply of water and for the disposal of domestic waste are made normally in the United Kingdom by means of a fixed rate charge levied on each householder according to the value of his house. Having paid this compulsory fixed charge the householder is free without any extra charge to run as much water as he likes and to put out as much waste as he likes for the municipal dustman to collect. But the provision of extra water and the disposal of extra waste are by no means costless activities. It would certainly be technically possible to instal domestic water meters and to charge according to the quantity of water used and to have the solid wastes put out for disposal weighed and to charge according to the amount involved. The question arises whether the improvement in the pricing mechanism would be worth the additional cost involved.

A final example may be taken from the supply of electricity to domestic users.  The cost of providing the current is much greater at the peak hours of consumption than at times when the demand is slack.  The simplest system of charging is to charge according to the amount of current used without any regard to the question whether the current has been costly or cheap to provide.  A somewhat more sophisticated system is to supply current at a low price separately for certain heating installations on a time switch which cuts off the supply at times of peak load.  A still more sophisticated system would be to supply all currents on a single but elaborate meter which would automatically record a variable charge per unit of current consumed according to the rest of the total load on the supply system.  At what point of refinement of charging does the additional cost of metering outweigh the advantages of the additional accuracy of the pricing system?

In fact in every concern, both public and private, the operation of the pricing system will involve a cost—at the very minimum some cost of cash registers, accounting clerks, invoices, etc. etc.  In every case there is a balance to be sought between the advantages of a more accurate pricing system and the costs of its administration.  In every case the pricing system because it is costly will be less refined than would otherwise be the case.  Everywhere there is some element of externality due to the 'market-organisation-cost'.  It is an arbitrary matter where one draws the line and considers a significant externality problem to exist.

### (4) *The Fiscal Set of Conditions*

Taxes and subsidies may, of course, be set by the government on various activities in order to reduce or to offset externalities.  I shall discuss this possibility at length in Chapter IV.  But taxes may be imposed for other reasons, for example, to raise revenue for some objects of public expenditure or, together with subsidies, to redistribute income and purchasing power.  Where a tax or a subsidy is imposed on an activity in which there was no pre-existing other cause of divergence between marginal value and marginal cost, a tax will cause marginal value to remain above marginal cost and *vice versa* with a subsidy on the activity.  This will give rise to externalities.

If I increase at the margin my purchase of a commodity subject to such a tax, the value of the unit of the commodity to me is represented by the price of the product including the tax ; the cost of the factors used to produce it is represented by the price excluding the tax ; the additional revenue to the government due to my purchase represents an excess of value over cost and there is a real-income gain which accrues to those who gain from the increased governmental tax revenue. Who these gainers will be depends upon what the government does with its budget surplus. But by purchasing another unit of this taxed commodity I have given rise to an external economy which will be to someone's net benefit.

A progressive income tax, imposed in order to redistribute net incomes more equally, provides a good illustration of the principle. Progressive lump-sum taxes, i.e. poll taxes fixed in amount for each individual but scaled according to his earning capacity rather than to his actual earnings, are theoretically ideal for purposes of redistribution. They take more from the rich man than from the poor man without altering the marginal relationship between earnings and net retained income from an additional effort to earn. The potentially rich man pays a high lump-sum in taxation but can retain £1 for every additional £1 which he chooses to earn.

But such a tax system is not a practicable possibility. The problem of assessing earning capacity as contrasted with actual earnings in insoluble. A progressive income tax must be assessed on actual earnings. So the rich man for every £1 which he adds to his gross income will keep say 30p. the remaining 70p. going to the government.

If such a man does decide to earn more he confers an external economy on those who will benefit from the increased budgetary revenue. The value to the consumers of his marginal product is £1 ; the cost of the additional effort to him is 30p. ; the difference is a real-income externality, represented by the excess of the value of what he produces over the cost to him of the additional effort.

## (5) *The Monopolistic Set of Conditions*

Wherever there is an element of monopoly which is exploited for the profit of the monopolist, there will be some restriction of output which will raise the price charged for the good or service above its marginal cost. Monopolistic conditions may result from institutional or legal impediments to the entry of new competitors or from economies of large-scale production of such a magnitude that there is not room in the market for a large number of competitors. But whatever its cause, the result of monopolistic conditions which are exploited for profit will be a marginal divergence of selling price over cost. The way in which this will lead to externalities has already been discussed in Chapter I and I will not repeat the analysis here.

Exactly similar conditions result from the existence of monopsonistic conditions. Whereever a buyer by restricting his purchases can beat down the price of what he buys, a search for profit on his part will lead to some restriction of his purchases with a resulting depression of the price to the seller below the marginal value of the thing bought to the buyer. An increase in the quantity bought by a monopsonist, just as an increase in the quantity sold by a monopolist, will lead to an external economy.

In the real world in a very large number of markets there is some monopolistic or monopsonist element. It is a question of degree to decide from the point of view of public policy at what point one takes notice and says that the externality is on a scale which calls for some remedial action.

### (6) *The Moulding-of-Preferences Set of Conditions*

I come finally to the most puzzling set of the lot. There are many activities such as commercial advertising, to say nothing of political speeches, religious sermons, and university lectures, which alter citizens' tastes. Take the case of commercial advertisement. The advertiser takes a decision in which I play no part but which causes me to prefer commodity X to Y instead of Y to X. Am I better off or not? The advertisement may have stimulated an entirely new desire in my heart and I now desire to have X, which is nevertheless out of my reach. My consequent discontent may make me unhappy. But perhaps, particularly if it is the result of a sermon and not of a television advertisement, it is a divine discontent which will make me strive for better and higher things, making me for the first time unhappy to realise what a miserable creature I am.

An induced change in a utility function is not the same thing as sharing a variable in a utility function with some other person or persons. But it undoubtedly falls within the wider definition of an externality given in Chapter I ; it is an effect which is to my benefit or damage due to an action in deciding on which I played no part.

But having reached these big and fundamental ethical issues, the economist may judge that he has reached the boundary of his subject and may be well advised to fall silent, leaving others to take up the theme.

# III. The Internalisation
of Real-Income Externalities

II. The Internalisation
of Real-Income Externalities

An externality, as we have defined it, occurs when someone is seriously affected for good or ill as a result of a decision to which he or she was not a party. A first obvious way to attempt to improve matters is to rearrange the institutions of society in such a way that the affected person does become a party in reaching any decision which affects his interests seriously. In other words, one may seek a reform of institutions which internalises the externalities. Such institutions for joint internalised decision-making can take many forms : a family ; a social club ; a business company corporation or partnership ; a local government ; a central government—to name only some of the most obvious types.

Let us start by giving two examples. Consider once more the pool of oil which lies under the land of a large number of independent land-owners ; each of whom will be tempted to pump out the oil beneath his own land at an uneconomic rate in order to lay his hands on it before his neighbour has pumped it away. Suppose now that the landowners are brought together in the formation of a joint company to which they surrender their ownership of the oil beneath their lands. The manager of the company could be instructed to pump the oil at the most economic rate so as to maximise the profits of the company, and thereby each landowner could as a shareholder in a single company obtain a higher income from the oil than before.

There is an obvious powerful incentive voluntarily to create such institutions for real-income externalities. In the case of the oil pool, by getting together all the landowners can simultaneously be better off than they would otherwise be ; and for this reason they will have a powerful motive to get together and form the oil company.

This does not mean that there are no distributional problems or conflicts of interest in setting up institutions to internalise real-income externalities. On the contrary, although in a particular case it may be possible to rearrange matters so as to make everyone concerned better off than before, it may not be easy to reach agreement on the choice of the particular new arrangement. One new arrangement may give all or most of the benefit to A and little or none to B, while another new arrangement may give little to A and much to B.

This situation gives rise to the acute bargaining difficulties which I have already mentioned in Chapter II. Suppose that the oil pool company is in the process of formation and that all the landowners except one recalcitrant individual have already joined forces. If the recalcitrant non-co-operator can drain as quickly as he pleases as much oil as he pleases from all his neighbours, the oil-pool company will lose its attraction for the others unless he also can be persuaded to join. He can, therefore, hope to obtain ultimately an unduly large share of the total gain. But every landowner may feel tempted to play this role of the recalcitrant non-co-operator. This sort of bargaining deadlock, together with the mere problem of organisation if there are a large number of landlords concerned, may well mean that some form of compulsory governmental action is required if the oil-pool merger is to be successfully achieved.

The example which I have just given is very straightforward in the sense that it involves only a conflict of interest about the share of the given total money profit obtainable from a joint exploitation of the oil reserve. In many cases of institutional arrangements for the internalisation of externalities the issues and conflicts of interest are more complicated and subtle, as in the following example.

Suppose that the residential area of a new town is being planned. Shall the town have large public parks and gardens with little or no private gardens ? Or shall the town be planned with the same density of housing but with no public gardens, leaving the various private dwellings to have private gardens of varied shapes and sizes ? If the public-garden solution is adopted, then for the upkeep of the public garden every resident will have to pay taxes on some uniform principle, which for practical reasons will not be able to take into account individual preferences for gardens. With the private-garden solution each resident will pay for the upkeep—or neglect—of his own garden. With the private-garden solution there are many externalities. My well kept garden will give pleasure to the neighbours. Your neglected garden will not merely be a squalid eyesore for the neighbours, but the weeds which you fail to control will invade and spoil my beautiful garden. The public-garden solution will internalise these externalities and thereby a given excellence of garden will be achieved at a lower cost per acre—the control of weeds, for example, being cheaper because it is universal.

On the other hand the public-garden solution will mean that everyone must have, as it were, the same amount of garden. This can give rise to a very real conflict of interest. Some residents may have a low demand for gardens, either because they live indoor lives or perhaps because they are poor and cannot afford it. With the private-garden solution these persons would choose to live in houses with no garden, and would spend on other things what they saved on the cost of upkeep of a garden. With the public-garden solution they would be forced to pay taxes on some uniform principle to enjoy the uniform amount of garden space.

Of course, a private garden is not a perfect substitute for a public garden so that some communally minded residents may in principle prefer the public-garden solution while other individualistic people may in principle prefer the private garden solution. But quite apart from this difference, conflict of interest may arise because some people have a high and others a low demand for garden space and garden beauty whether of a public or private nature.

Which solution should be adopted will, of course, be affected by the technological problems involved. How great are the external diseconomies of your neglect of weeds in your garden, i.e. how much is the cost of producing a good garden reduced by the adoption of the public-garden solution ? But the point which I wish to emphasise is that the solution which *will* be sought and—a quite different matter—the solution which *should* be sought will depend upon one's answer to much more basic problems of human society. How should collective decisions be reached ? Above all how much weight should be given, and in what manner and by what means, to the fact that the conflict of interest may be one concerned with the distribution of income between the rich and the poor—in my example between the rich who can afford and want a pleasant environment and the poor who would rather have resources devoted to more immediate and pressing necessities ?

I fear that I cannot attempt to give any final answer to these basic political-social-moral issues. I must content myself with pointing out one or two factors which are relevant in reaching any final decisions.

A first distinction of basic importance in considering the best structure of institutions designed to internalise externalities is whether the externalities which are internalised must be treated on a large scale or can be treated on a small scale. As an example of small-scale treatment one may instance the carpenter whom I hired at the beginning of Chapter I to mend my table ; the noise which he made affected only those in the very near neighbourhood. In such a case there can, therefore, be a very large number of small local authorities with different rules about the noises made by the hammering of carpenters. As an instance of a necessarily large-scale treatment one may cite the decision as to whether the country should possess nuclear weapons or not ; we must all live either with or without them.

A second distinction of importance is whether membership of the institution which internalises externalities is voluntary or compulsory. At the one extreme a citizen is completely free to decide whether he will join a social club or not. At the other extreme, a citizen of any given country cannot escape the laws and regulations of the central government of his country. But there is no sharp dividing line between the voluntary and the compulsory institutions ; there is merely a cost, running from zero to infinity, in changing one's membership of institutions for collective decision-making. A man may legally be completely free to leave his employment with a particular firm whose rules and regulations he dislikes and to take employment elsewhere ; but if the firm with which he is working is the only firm in the region which employs persons with his particular skill and training, this freedom may be more apparent than real. On the other hand, although obedience to the rules of the government under which one lives is compulsory, yet, at the cost of changing one's residence, one can change one's government, a cost which may be moderate if it is a question of moving from the authority of one small local government to that of another ; which will be heavy if it is a question of moving from one country to another ; and which—until inter-planetary travel becomes feasible—will be infinite when we have established a world government from whose jurisdiction no-one can escape.

A third matter of extreme importance is the nature of the rules for reaching collective decisions within the institutions which internalise externalities.

One possible decision-making rule is that no action shall be taken except with unanimous agreement of the members of the institution. Such a rule puts an enormous weight on the *status quo*. No action will be easy to take which makes any one member of the organisation worse off, however great the advantage of the action concerned to some other mem-

48

ber or members of the group and however just and proper such a redistribution may seem to the members whose interests are not at stake. Moreover, such a rule does nothing to solve, it merely postpones, the bargaining problems which arise in reaching joint decisions. Thus if there are two possible courses of action, action I giving much benefit to one group of members, group A, and little benefit to another group, group B, whereas action II gives much benefit to B and little to A, a unanimity rule may mean that it is impossible for the society as a whole to agree on the choice between action I and action II.

An alternative form of decision-making rule is to abide by the result of a majority vote of the members of the institution. Here there are two very well known disadvantages.

First, it may be possible for an unscrupulous majority to use their voting power to fleece a minority group.

Second, it may in certain circumstances lead to a very unstable form of decision-making. Suppose that there are three groups of members A, B, and C each one of which contains less than 50 % of the total membership, and that these groups have the following preference orders for three possible policies I, II, and III :

| A | B | C |
|---|---|---|
| I | II | III |
| II | III | I |
| III | I | II |

Suppose we start with policy I in operation. A will be very happy ; but B and C can form a coalition and vote for III in preference to I, making C very happy. But A and B can then get together and vote for II in preference to III, giving B his first choice. But then A and C can vote for I in preference to II, restarting the whole merry-go-round of unstable decisions.

A third possible procedure is for some system of weighted voting whereby if there are, say, three possible courses of action, I, II and III, each member of the institution can give 3 votes to his first choice, 2 to his second, and 1 to his third. The action with the greatest number of votes will then be chosen. In the example which I have just given this would lead to a choice of actions I, II, or III according as whether group A, group B, or group C was the largest group. This method has in my opinion much to recommend it. But its proper functioning depends upon putting up for a simultaneous vote all the possible alternative lines of action—a totally impracticable requirement for any institution with any degree of complication of activities.

A fourth possible procedure is for the decisions of the institution which internalises externalities to be taken by some authoritarian manager or controller or guardian on behalf of the members. Quite apart from violent and forcible dictatorships there are two quite voluntary and democratic ways in which such a regime may be set up. In the first place, the members of the institution may take the original constituent joint decision that they will accept the decisions of a governor, the constitutional method of appointment of this governor being unanimously agreed on the original formation of the institution. Alternatively there may be a large number of independent institutions each with an externally established authoritarian governor, but individuals may be free to choose their governor not by choosing a governor for their own particular institution but by choosing which institution they will join and thus which governor they will obey. I will give some examples of this in due course.

In view of these distinctions are there any generalisations which one can make about what forms of institution with what rules for collective decision-making are appropriate for what kinds of externality ?

Let us first consider a voluntary institution coping with a small-scale externality. There are, for example, in a given town a large number of housing estates. In some the rooms are all insulated heavily against noise ; in these houses, at the extra cost of the noise insulation, musicians who want to make much musical noise without being interrupted by each other's noise may live together in musicianly companionship. Other estates have no noise insulation ; but some of them have rules prohibiting the playing of musical instruments and here those who simply want quiet may live. Other estates have no noise insulation and no rules against musical instruments and here those who like to live in a jolly atmosphere of transistor radios and pop music may live happily together.

In such circumstances the obvious way to cope with externalities is to promote the setting up of a large number of competing institutions to cover this externality in different ways. In such cases it does not matter greatly whether the decision-making process is authoritarian or not. Indeed the various housing estates in my example could all be set up by commercial companies which simply laid down from outside the rules for all potential tenants. If a great variety of estates is available, the individual citizen can choose the rules under which he lives not by taking part

50

in the decision-making process in the institution to which he belongs but by selecting the institution to which he chooses to belong.

The same is true of the small competing company. If there are a large number of competing small employers in a district, the worker can choose his employer. Workers' participation in the running of the concern may be easier to organise where the concern is small ; but it will be less necessary where there are many competing firms, since the worker can influence his employer by preferring an employer with one set of working rules to an employer with another set of working rules.

The position is very different with a single large-scale organisation. The worker on a national railway network may be free to leave his employment ; and it may even be that he could readily find another job which required the same degree of skill and effort and offered the same pay and prospects. But he may simply like being a railway man. In such a case the process of decision-making on the national railway system is of importance to him ; workers' participation may be more difficult to organise on so large a scale, but it is more important than in the case of the small competitive firm. The fact that an institution must be on a large scale inevitably implies that there is a considerable cost of movement into or out of it. Thus the railway man's desire to remain a railway man is a psychic cost of movement out of the railway institution.

But largeness of scale of operations is not the only reason for cost of movement. If mother and father are really joined together in holy matrimony until death doth them part, the cost of movement out of the family institution is infinite. It then makes a great deal of difference whether father who likes quiet dictatorially bans the radio or whether mother who likes pop music insists on playing the radio all day or whether a more decent process of collective choice results in an agreement that mother shall enjoy the radio when father is out at work. In such a small institution based on goodwill it may not be too difficult to reach reasonable rules to cope with externalities.

But where the institution is both large-scale and movement out is impossible the rules for decision making become both important and difficult. The decisions of the national government are the outstanding cases in this category. Whether or not the country should possess an atom bomb is a matter which will inevitably affect every citizen and the most satisfactory process of decision making is notoriously difficult to find.

I cannot give you any final solution of this problem. But I have one observation to make about it. In my view the ideal society would be one in which each citizen developed a real split personality, acting selfishly in the market place and altruistically at the ballot box. It is, for example, perfectly possible for a rich and influential man to arrange his affairs within the existing framework of law to the best advantage of himself, of his family, of his club, and of any business concern which he may help to direct and, at the same time, to urge through the political process a change in the law which will be to the disadvantage of his family or his business but to the greater advantage of other members of society. If this were not so, the prospects for a decent society would indeed be dim. It is, for example, only by such 'altruistic' political action that there can be any alleviation of 'poverty' in a society in which the 'poor' are in a minority.

Thus a rich man can work politically for a system of taxation which will affect adversely all rich men and will result in a more equal distribution of income and wealth, or a business man can vote for a legislative change which will impose a new charge on all the firms (including his own) in some competitive industry which is causing a problem of pollution.

Such a state of affairs would get the best division of labour, as it were, in ordering the affairs of society. The individual citizen with his selfish preferences in the market place would be attending in the most efficient way to the welfare of those little atoms in society—himself, his family, his club, his business—about whose needs he is best informed. The statesmen whom he elects altruistically to be his political governors can attend to the details of setting that structure of legislative rules and taxes which will provide a framework within which the selfish atomic acts of the individual citizens in the market place will, through the hidden hand of the legislators, add up to a just and efficient total system.

But even if we could get everyone to act altruistically at the ballot box, different citizens would have different views as to what does constitute justice in society. We would need in addition some humdrum work-a-day rule for selecting from among these conflicting ideas about justice and about the ultimate aims of the Good Society some set of rules which counted heads rather than breaking them. And one should never forget that there is no more potent cause of broken heads than differences of ideology.

Thus for the Good Society we need a combination of economics, ethics, and politics : first, an *economically* efficient selfishness *à la* Adam Smith in the market place ; second, an *ethical* search for justice to guide the formation of individuals' preferences as between different governmental policies ; and third some humdrum *political* rules of voting to choose between any resulting conflicting views about such policies.

But we are not there yet ; and until our choices of public policy are guided more altruistically than at present, we cannot afford to promote pure selfishness in the market place. Meanwhile I must leave you to decide how to make the best of a bad job.

# IV. The Governmental Regulation of Externalities

For the reasons discussed in Chapter III we cannot rely upon voluntary clubs or companies to internalise all important externalities. Governmental compulsory intervention will often be necessary. Such intervention can take either of two forms : (a) the government can take over and itself run some line of activity such as police, defense, etc. or (b) it can leave the activity to private initiative but regulate, by taxation or otherwise, the resulting private activities in such a way as to counteract any externalities involved in those private activities.

When the government adopts course (a), this is a case of the institutional internalisation of externalities discussed in Chapter III. In the present Chapter IV I intend to discuss certain problems which arise when the government adopts course (b), namely the regulation of the activities of other independent bodies. In particular should governmental control of externalities arising in the private sector of the economy take the form of prohibitions and of direct quantitative regulations of certain activities or the form of taxes to discourage and of subsidies to encourage activities which create external diseconomies or economies ?

Let us consider the case of a factory belching smoke and polluting the atmosphere or emptying some industrial effluent into a river and polluting the water. The first simple point to make is that it is not necessarily in the social interest to prohibit all the pollution. A moderate amount of pollution may do little damage to society, whereas the cost of complete abatement of the pollution might be exceedingly high. There is an optimal level of pollution which is illustrated in Figure I.

Suppose that in the absence of any control an industry would find it convenient to emit OO' units of pollution. The curve OC measures the increasing marginal damage done to society as the amount of pollution increases. But pollution abatement costs something, and the stricter the

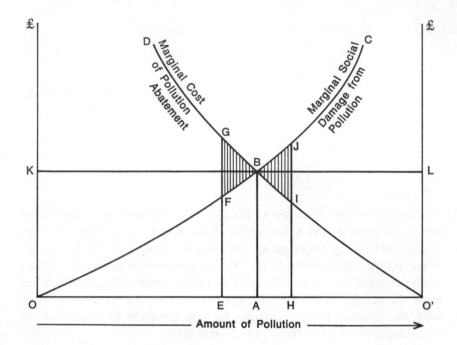

**Figure I**

abatement the higher probably the marginal cost. The rising marginal cost of pollution abatement is shown by the curve O'D. OA, determined by the point of intersection of these two curves, is the optimum amount of pollution. If the pollution were restricted from OA to OE, the shaded area FGB would represent an additional excess of costs of abatement over the value of the reduction of the damage done to society. If the amount of pollution were increased from OA to OH, the shaded area IJB would represent an excess of the value of the increased damage done to society over the saving in costs of abatement.

The curve O'D of the marginal cost of pollution abatement is a fairly definite cost curve which can be expressed in £'s. A reduction in their emission of pollution from OO' to, say, OH will add some fairly precise amount to the costs of the industrialists concerned. It may not be easy for the governmental authority to discover this figure in advance (I shall have more to say on that problem later) ; but the figure itself is a reasonably definite one. It is the cost of abatement of pollution by an amount O'H by whatever means is cheapest to the industrialist concerned.

58

But the marginal social damage curve OC, which must also be estimated in £'s by the governmental authority concerned in order to compare it with the pollution abatement cost curve OD' presents difficulties of a different order altogether. Let us suppose that we are dealing with the belching of smoke by a producer A which soils the laundry of the neighbouring housewives B, C, D, etc.—the classical example which we considered in Chapter II (1). We are assuming that because of the bargaining and organisational problems which we discussed in Chapter II (1) we cannot leave the outcome to a joint decision to be reached voluntarily by A, B, C, and D. The control of the emission of smoke by A is to be done by some governmental regulation. How does the government set about estimating in £'s the value of the damage done to B, C, and D by the smoke which A emits ?

The first question for the government to decide is whether it should do its sums on the basis that the clean air belongs in the first place to A or to B, C, and D. If the clean air is treated as belonging to A, then the government must think in terms of the amounts of money which B, C, and D would offer to A to persuade him to abate the smoke nuisance by a given amount. If B, C, and D are poor, then this sum may be very small, since they simply do not possess the means to offer much. But if the clean air is taken as belonging to B, C, and D (which to me personally would appear to be the preferable assumption) then even if B, C, and D are poor, the amount which A would have to offer them to put up with a given degree of smoke nuisance might be quite high. B, C, and D might need a large increase in their income to compensate them for the smoke, even though their incomes were so low that they could not possibly offer A much in order to get rid of the smoke.

These considerations raise the question whether, if B, C, and D are poor and A is rich, one should not go further than merely assume that the clean air belongs to B, C, and D. Ought one not to put a greater weight on £1 of social damage than on £1 of abatement cost, since a £1 which must be paid by A to B, C, and D to induce them to take the smoke means more in utility to poor B, C, and D than it does to rich A ?

This question raises a basic issue which I cannot discuss on this occasion. There would, however, be a certain inconsistency in a system which does not compensate for inequalities in ordinary private market transactions but insists on doing so in these collective decisions. If we allow the rich man to outbid the poor man in the private markets for food, clothing, heating, housing, etc. why should we not allow him to do so in

59

the collective 'market' for clean air ? Surely, it may be argued, the correct policy is by fiscal means to redistribute income in whatever manner one considers to be just and efficient, and then to count £1 as £1 in private and collective transactions, from whatever citizen the £1 may come or to whatever citizen the £1 be paid. On the other hand, it may be argued that so long as the State does not adopt a general fiscal solution to obtain the optimal distribution of income there is no reason why it should not make some partial move in the right direction when it is considering the regulation of externalities by putting more weight on the £1 of any poor man than on the £1 of any rich man who may be affected by the regulation.

Apart from this basic issue there are all the difficulties of assessing the value of social damage done which have been discussed by implication in Chapter II (1).

First, even if one decided that the value of the social damage done should be assessed at the amount which B, C, and D would have to be paid to put up with the given degree of smoke nuisance, how does one set about estimating this man ? For the bargaining reasons discussed in Chapter II (1), Mrs. B, C, and D will have every incentive to overstate their demands and there is no straightforward market mechanism to test at what price each of them would in fact be ready to sell their rights to clean air.

Second, as in the case of the use of a pesticide such as DDT, the damage done may be in the fairly distant future, and may in any case be uncertain. How does one estimate the *present* value of an *uncertain* damage to *future* generations ? This also is a problem which it is not possible to discuss properly on this occasion.

What is clear, however, is that in order to make any reasonable attempt to grapple with the problems of regulating pollution the governmental authorities concerned must make some attempt to compare in the same monetary units the cost of pollution abatement and the present value of the social damage done by the pollution ; that both of these and in particular the latter will be a matter of considerable doubt and uncertainty ; and indeed that the value of the social damage done will have in many cases to be set at a figure determined in a rather arbitrary hunch like manner.

Suppose then that the abatement costs and the value of the social damage have been estimated in the best manner possible. Let us return to Figure I. By what type of regulation should the government attempt to achieve the restriction of the amount of pollution to OA ?  One method would be by a direct quantitative regulation whereby the government allocated individual permits to pollute to the individual firms concerned, the total amount of pollution permitted by the sum of these individual licenses being set at OA.  Another method would be to impose a tax at the rate AB or O'L on each unit of pollution emitted.  Starting from O' each firm, by abating pollution by one more unit, would save more in the reduction of tax than it would add to the cost of abatement so long as its marginal cost of pollution abatement were lower than the tax per unit of pollution, i.e. for the industry as a whole so long as the curve O'D was below the tax per unit of pollution, AB.  To reduce pollution below the amount OA would mean that the saving in tax on pollution was less than the added costs of abatement.

There are some very substantial advantages in operating by means of a tax rather than a quantitative regulation.  If there are a number of different firms polluting a river and it is desirable to restrict the total amount of pollution, the imposition of a tax per unit of pollution, leaving each firm free to decide how much pollution it will cause, will produce a given reduction in pollution at a minimal cost.  Those firms which find it cheap to abate pollution will restrict their pollution much more than those firms for which pollution abatement is costly.  A given total reduction in pollution will thus be obtained at the lowest possible cost.

Moreover a tax on pollution will leave each polluter complete freedom of choice in the method, as well as in the amount, of pollution abatement. Research and development can be devised in a quite unrestricted manner to discover new and cheaper methods of abatement.

The efficiency of using a tax-cum-price mechanism for controlling pollution becomes even clearer when there are a number of different technical methods of control all of which may be used simultaneously to contribute to the problem.  Let us suppose that there are the following five ways of coping with the purification of a water supply which is dirtied by some industry's effluent :

(1)  The amount of pollution which the industry produces may be restricted.

(2)  The river authority may be able by storing water in reservoirs during the rainy season to increase the average flow of clean water through the river and thus dilute the pollutant.

(3) A public water supply company can purify the polluted water for supply to consumers.

(4) The demand of consumers for purified water may be restricted.

(5) Some large-scale private consumers may be able to apply their own filtering apparatus to the polluted river water.

By an appropriate use of taxes and prices these various methods of pollution control can be combined into the most efficient whole. The interrelations between these prices and taxes is examined in a more precise manner in Appendix A. The following is only a very general sketch of the interconnections between them. The tax authority must set a rate of tax on the industrial effluent which corresponds to the additional cost of private and public purification which would result from an additional unit of pollutant. The water authority must set a price at which it will meet the consumers' demands for clean water and must adjust this price up or down to equate it to its own marginal cost of purifying water. The river authority must adjust its expenditure on increasing the flow of river water, until the cost of increasing the flow is in proper relation to the tax set on industrial effluent. The consumers of clean water can then be left to determine their demand from the public water authority and their own supply from their own filters. This system of control through prices and taxes has all the familiar advantages of a decentralised price mechanism. Everyone minds the business which he is best fitted to mind ; and the efficiency guides to co-ordinate these independent decisions are the signals flashed from one sector of the system to another through the ruling prices and rates of taxation.

There is another important general argument for controlling external diseconomies by charging taxes or other levies rather than by direct regulation. In modern society it is necessary for the State to raise large sums of tax revenue for the finance of expenditure on pure public goods (such as defense, law and order) and for the redistribution of income and wealth. As I have already argued in Chapter II (4), it is impossible to do this by the ideal form of progressive poll taxes, which would have the desired incidence from the distributional point of view without causing divergences between marginal values and marginal costs and thus without being themselves the occasion for undesirable externalities. But it is very different with taxes which are levied on particular activities for the express purpose of closing the otherwise existing divergences between marginal costs and marginal values which would be associated with these activities. Such taxes kill two birds with one stone : they directly reduce the particular externalities which they are directly designed to counteract and at the same time they raise revenue for the finance of other necessary governmental expenditures, thus reducing the need to impose revenue—raising taxes which would themselves introduce or intensify certain other externalities.

In many cases it may be possible to achieve a similar immediate result either by taxing an activity or by subsidising a reduction in that activity. In terms of Figure I as we have already argued, a tax of AB = O'L on each unit of pollutant would give the polluter an inducement to reduce his pollution from OO' to OA. But a subsidy of AB = O'L on each unit by which pollution was reduced below OO' would have a similar effect ; the polluter starting at O' would gain more in subsidy than he would lose in the cost of pollution abatement so long as the marginal cost of pollution abatement was less than the subsidy AB.

As a general principle the taxation of pollution is to be preferred to the subsidisation of non-pollution. If one offers a subsidy to non-pollution which is open to all new concerns which may be set up in the industry or activity concerned, one will have in each case to estimate what would have been the degree of pollution if one had not subsidised its removal in order in the case of each new concern to have a benchmark from which to measure the degree of pollution abatement. Quite apart from this difficulty one would in any case be giving a subsidy to a polluting industry as a whole and would be uneconomically encouraging new entrants into that industry.

But in the case of an existing concern in the industry which is already emitting a given level of pollution one has a benchmark from which to operate ; and if one is introducing anti-pollution measures completely *de novo* it may seem right and proper to compensate the particular concern for the cost to it of the new measures which are being imposed. This could be achieved by paying to existing concerns a subsidy for pollution abatement at a rate equal in Figure I to AB or O'L which would give the concerns an additional net profit of O'BL, the difference between the total subsidy ABLO' and the total abatement cost ABO' ; and this could be offset by charging the concerns in lump-sum taxes an amount equal to O'BL. Or the same result could be achieved by imposing a tax per unit of pollution equal to AB which would raise a tax revenue of OKBA (i.e. the tax rate AB on the remaining pollution OA) and would impose a net cost to the concerns of OKBO' (i.e. the tax payment OKBA plus the abatement cost ABO') ; and this could be offset by lump-sum subsidies to the concerns amounting to OKBO'. In both cases the concerns have the same inducement to abate pollution to OA and the government bears the net cost of pollution abatement ABO'.

One can thus always operate by means of a general tax on pollution, compensating, if one thinks fit, the existing firms for the additional cost thus imposed on them by means of a lump-sum compensation payment. But whatever be the rights and wrongs of such compensation to existing concerns for the cost of newly introduced measures of pollution abatement there is no case for the subsidisation of pollution avoidance rather than for the taxation of pollution in the general case which covers new firms. Not only does it encourage uneconomically the new entry of concerns into these polluting activities ; but it will involve the raising of more tax revenue by other fiscal means rather than itself making a contribution to the raising of tax revenue and thus indirectly making a contribution to the avoidance of those divergences between marginal costs and values which the raising of tax revenue in general involves.

There are many ways in which this choice between the taxation of the creation of pollution and the subsidisation of the avoidance of pollution may show itself. For example, we all now realise that motor transport in large cities is causing intolerable congestion, noise, danger to life and limb, and atmospheric pollution. We all realise that private transport causes much more trouble per passenger-mile than does public transport. Both cause these troubles, but private transport causes more trouble than does public transport. The proper conclusion is to tax both forms of transport but to encourage public transport relatively to private transport by taxing private transport much more heavily than public transport. For the reasons which I have just given, it is a false conclusion to leave the taxation of private transport where it is, but to subsidise public transport in order to attract passengers from the private to the public sector.

A tax imposed per unit of pollution emitted is not the only way of using the price mechanism to regulate pollution. If it is considered possible and desirable to control the quantity of pollution emitted by each polluter, the following procedure might be adopted. The authority concerned determines the total amount of pollution which shall be permitted —e.g. the total amount of some industrial effluent which all the industrial concerns together shall be allowed to discharge at a particular point into a given river. Licenses to pollute up to this amount are then put up to auction, so that the total permitted amount of pollution is distributed over all the industrial concerns in such a manner that at the closing auction price per unit of licensed pollution each concern has in fact itself decided how much pollution it is economic for it to emit.

This auctioning of licenses to pollute has many of the same basic features as a system of a tax levied per unit of pollutant. Both raise revenue by charging for an external diseconomy, and both enable the price mechanism to be used to determine the cheapest and most efficient way of obtaining a reduction in pollution. The basic difference is that in the case of the straightforward tax the authority first guesses what is the optimum tax and can then judge whether some revision of the tax is desirable in the light of the resulting quantity of pollution, whereas with the auctioning of licenses the authority first guesses what is the desirable quantity of pollution to permit and then can judge whether, in the light of the price which polluters will offer for licenses to pollute, it should increase or decrease the licenses which in future it puts up for auction.

The choice between these two procedures must be influenced by what the authorities consider to be the shape of the curves of marginal social damage and of marginal abatement cost. In Figures II and III the correct levy to charge per unit of pollutant is in both cases O'L, which will induce the polluters to go in for the optimal amount of pollution abatement O'A.

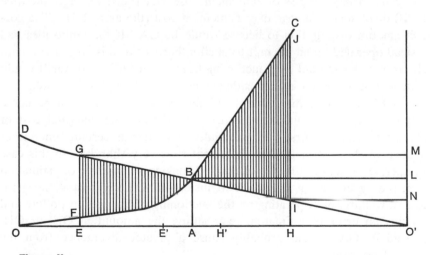

**Figure II**

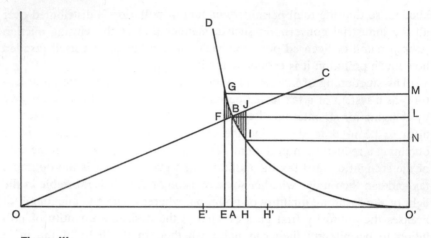

**Figure III**

In Figure II the marginal abatement cost rises at a uniform gradual rate whereas the marginal social damage rises at first gradually but then reaches a danger level at which it rises very rapidly. In this case a false estimate of the proper tax, e.g. a tax of O'N or of O'M instead of O'L, will cause a large excess of abatement cost over social damage (the area FGB) or of social damage over abatement cost (the area BJI). The correct amount of pollution to license would be OA. If the authorities had instead operated by an attempt to auction licences to this correct amount, an error in the amount (e.g. auctioning licenses for OE' or for OH') would probably have caused a smaller divergence from the optimum result.

In Figure III on the other hand the marginal social damage curve slopes upwards at a uniform gentle rate, whereas the marginal cost of abatement rises at first very gradually but after a certain amount of abatement the cost of further abatement rises very sharply. In this case to operate by setting the rate of tax and making some error of estimation (e.g. setting the tax at O'N or O'M instead of O'L) will cause no great loss of welfare, but operating by the auctioning of licences to pollute and making an error of estimation (e.g. setting the amount at OE' or OH' instead of OA) would probably cause a greater divergence from the optimal position.

66

The distinctions which I have just drawn between the cases in which a straightforward tax, levy, or charge per unit of pollution is to be preferred and the cases in which the auctioning of the rights to a given quantity of pollution is a better method should not be confused with a different, important, but purely administrative distinction. For administrative reasons it may be much cheaper to enforce a regulation which prohibits a polluter from emitting more than a given amount of pollution rather than to levy a tax per unit of pollutant which is emitted. The levying of the tax may involve the installation of some sophisticated metering device in each concern and its policing by the tax authority, whereas the regulation of a maximum permitted quantity may be monitored by a simpler device which merely indicates whether the amount of pollution has exceeded a stated level or in some cases may be adequately policed by a system of spot checks by visiting inspectors to ensure that the limit is not being exceeded.

This administrative consideration can presumably be met by auctioning licenses to emit pollution up to a given level and then, by a system of spot checks or whatever may be the appropriate method of monitoring, ensuring that no polluter is exceeding the limit to which his license entitles him. But it may at first sight appear that this could give rise to a conflict of considerations. Suppose that in a given instance the shape of the marginal abatement cost and social damage curves are as in Figure III so that it would appear wise to proceed by means of a tax per unit of pollutant, but that the administrative considerations are in favour of regulating the maximum amount of pollution to be permitted to any given polluter. The conflict is in fact only an apparent one. In such a case one could proceed by issuing licenses to pollute, each license giving the right to pollute up to a given stated level, but instead of auctioning a given amount of such licenses one could sell at a given price however many such licenses any individual polluter might care to purchase at that price. In this case one would end up with a situation in which the administrative problem was to ensure that no polluter exceeded the maximum emission of pollution to which he was entitled, but in which he could choose whatever level of entitlement he thought best at the given charge per unit of entitlement.

We end up, therefore, with three methods of applying the price mechanism to the control of pollution :

(1) a straight tax, charge, or levy, per unit of pollution ;

(2) the auctioning of licenses which in total give right to a predetermined total emission of pollution ; and

(3) the sale, at a predetermined price per unit of permitted pollution, of rights to emit pollution up to any maximum chosen by the polluter.

The choice of the appropriate method depends upon both the administrative problems involved and also upon the view of the authorities concerned about the probable shape and position of the marginal curves of abatement costs and of social damage.

There are two further aspects of the administrative costs of controlling pollution that are relevant.

In the first place, it may often be much more expensive—or indeed technically impossible—to measure the amount of an actual pollutant, while it is possible and administratively much less expensive to measure the amount of some activity which is closely connected with the amount of pollutant produced and which, therefore, for the purpose of the control can act as a proxy for the pollutant itself.  For example, it may be easy to measure the input of a certain raw material into a factory, and the amount of the factory's output of a particular pollutant may be very closely related to the amount of this particular raw material which it uses. In such a case the best policy may be to control by tax or license the input of the material rather than the output of the pollutant.  The disadvantage of this device is that it removes all incentive to use existing means or to find new means to reduce the amount of pollution produced per unit of raw material used ; and thereby it may cause one possible means of pollution abatement to be totally disregarded.  But if the possibilities for such reduction of pollution output per unit of raw material input are small and if the administrative problems in monitoring raw material input are much smaller than in monitoring pollution output, it may be sensible to use raw material input as a proxy pollution output as a measure of control. However, the fact that for administrative reasons one may have to use a proxy for the actual pollutant in no way lessens the advantages of using the price mechanism (in the form of a tax or of a charge for a license) for the control of the proxy.

A second possible administrative problem does, however, mean that direct quantitative regulation may in some cases be preferable to the price mechanism.  To prohibit entirely some activity may be very much easier to monitor and enforce than to restrict the activity to some positive level

68

or to charge a tax per unit of that activity. Thus whether or not I play my radio at all may be much easier to determine than whether in playing my radio I have exceeded the creation of a certain restricted number of decibels of noise. Where for the early units of any polluting activity the cost of pollution abatement is less than or not much more than the social damage done, the loss of welfare caused by prohibition of the activity will be zero or at the worst very little. Where this is so and where at the same time prohibition is administratively much easier than other forms of control, complete prohibition is obviously the sensible policy.

But prohibition itself can take many forms, according to what is prohibited. Thus a regulation which says that in a certain block of dwellings radios may be played only between the hours of 10 a.m. to 10 p.m. is in fact a prohibition on making this particular sort of noise at all between the hours of 10 p.m. and 10 a.m. This may be a sensible possibility whereas a charge per decibel of radio noise which varied with the time of day might be wholly inoperable. Administrative considerations may well cause such regulations to be preferable to control through taxation or charging for licenses to produce a given quantity of the pollutant.

But administrative considerations apart there remain two very important classes of cases where for purely economic reasons regulations rather than price-mechanism charges may be needed.

The first type of case may be well illustrated by problems of town and country planning. In many countries a system of regulation by zoning is in operation. Certain activities may be developed only in certain scheduled areas. Thus certain areas are zoned for development of domestic dwellings, certain other areas for light industry, certain other areas for heavy industry, certain other areas for agriculture, and so on. One has no difficulty in seeing that there are important externalities which need to be controlled in one way or another. To take what has now become the classical example in this field, suppose an electric generating plant which belches much smoke and a laundry which needs clean air are situated in the same locality. Unless there is some governmental intervention the electrical generating plant will pour smoke into the air without reckoning the additional cost which that imposes on the neighbouring laundry.

But does one need to deal with this problem by a zoning regulation which states that electrical generation must take place in this zone while laundries must go to that other zone? Is it not sufficient in the way which I have argued at length to rely upon a tax mechanism? Suppose that one imposes a tax per unit of smoke on the electrical generating plant, the tax being adjusted so that the tax per additional unit of smoke is nicely adjusted to the additional laundering costs to which that additional unit of smoke gives rise. Will this not cope satisfactorily with the problem ? Will not the electrical generating plant be thereby induced to produce the optimal amount of smoke, i.e. to balance the gain from more electricity and incidentally more smoke against the additional costs of laundering which this involves ?

The answer, alas, may well be 'No' ; and in Appendix B I work out in detail a simple illustration of why this may be so. It is, of course, perfectly possible by such a tax to reach a situation which would be optimal if the electrical generating plant and the laundry had to remain together in the existing locality. Let us call this zone A. But suppose that there is some other locality (which we will call zone B) in which the electrical generating plant could operate or in which the laundry could operate, so that the two need not be side by side. If they do operate in separate zones, the externality disappears because there is no damage when either in a given locality there is no electrical generation (and therefore no smoke) or else no laundry (and therefore nothing for the smoke to damage). Zone B, the alternative locality, might well be one which would be less attractive than zone A to the electrical generating plant even if it were taxed at the appropriate marginal rate in zone A. Zone B might at the same time be less attractive than zone A to the laundry industry, even if it has to put up with the locally optimal amount of smoke from the electrical generating plant in zone A. Yet the community might be better off if one or the other moved to zone B.

This apparent paradox can be explained in the following way. Suppose that the electrical generating plant is required to move to zone B. It will *ex hypothesi* lose since the additional real costs of operating in the less advantageous zone B will be greater than the saving in the tax on smoke due to moving from zone A ; for if this were not so the plant would have chosen zone B of its own accord. The laundry which is left in zone A will gain in two ways. First, the cost of its existing activities will be reduced because of the absence of the smoke nuisance. This gain, however, is not a net gain to the community, since this cost was already being met by the tax on the electrical plant so long as it remained in zone A and the loss of this tax revenue to the government must be set against the reduction in the laundry's costs on its existing output. But there is a second gain to the laundry, namely the profit which it can now make on the expansion of its trade, since, with the reduction in its marginal costs due to the removal of the smoke nuisance, its marginal costs will now be below the marginal value of its output. This is a true gain to the community ; and it *may* exceed the loss incurred by the electricity plant in moving to the less favourable zone B.

Or suppose that it is the laundry which is required to move to zone B. It will incur a loss since *ex hypothesi* it prefers zone A, so that we may assume that what it gains in zone B by escaping the smoke nuisance to which it was subject in zone A is less than the other additional costs of operating in the less favourable locality. The electricity plant left in zone A will gain in two ways. First, it will no longer be subject to a smoke-nuisance tax. This gain is, however, not a net social gain, since the tax payer loses what the electricity plant gains. But the electricity plant can now expand its operations since the removal of the tax will have reduced the marginal cost of electricity generation below the value of the current to consumers. On this additional generation there is a real gain which may exceed the loss incurred by the laundry in moving to zone B.

Whether either and, if so, which activity should be moved to zone B is a question which can be answered only by a process of governmental cost-benefit analysis ; and the enforcement of the separation of the two activities, if their separation does turn out to be socially economic, can be achieved only by some form of governmental regulation. There is an unanswerable case for considering the desirability of regulation in order to enforce a structural separation of activities which will otherwise unnecessarily get into each other's way.

There is another class of cases, more familiar in the corpus of existing economic theory, in which governmental regulation may be needed in order to achieve the correct structure of activities. Where there are economies of large-scale production it may not be economic to produce some output of every conceivable product or quality of product. I have already alluded to this problem at the end of Chapter II (1), giving the example where it may be economic to produce only two car models, although there are six possible models from which the selection could be made. Which structure of the industry to choose, i.e. which two models to select, becomes in fact a matter of public choice. There is no reason to believe that the processes of the market will make the best choice. Indeed, it is not possible even to define the best choice until one has decided which is the right method of making a collective decision when different people have different and conflicting preferences.

In theory in such situations there is a case for some form of governmental regulation as to which activities should and which should not be operated. Once this structural choice has been made the marginal decisions as to the scale on which each permitted activity should be operated can be left to the price-cum-tax-cum-subsidy mechanism which we have already described.

Of course, there are many cases where the choice of the structure of activities by the chance of a *laissez-faire* market mechanism may not involve any serious social loss, and in which attempts to regulate the choice of activities might cost more in administrative costs and in the general interference to freedom caused by the bureaucratic process. In such cases it would be best not to intervene with a governmental regulation. The choice of which car models to produce may well be a case where it is best to leave ill alone.

But there are cases where regulation on these grounds may be desirable and indeed even quite inevitable. The problems of town and country planning by the zoning of activities which I have already discussed may in fact be redefined so as to fall into this category of cases. If we define electricity in zone A, electricity in zone B, laundering in zone A, and laundering in zone B as four different activities, then the zoning of such activities is simply a case of regulation of which activities are to be permitted and which are to be forbidden.

One other example may be useful. Let me revert to my illustration of the supply of purified water from some river which is polluted by some industrial effluent. Suppose that for technical reasons the individual filtering of the river water by private consumers is impossible. Only a public water supply to individual consumers is possible. What should be the quality of this water? How pure should it be? Or would it possibly be worth-while, in spite of the duplication of overhead costs of purification, piping etc., to have two separate water supplies to each house,— an expensive pure supply for drinking and cooking and a cheap less pure supply for watering the garden and flushing the lavatories? Such decisions cannot be reached by a simple application at the margin of the price-cum-tax-cum-subsidy mechanism. Some form of centralised estimation of the social costs and benefits involved and some form of centralised determination and enforcement of the number and structure of the activities to be performed is an inevitable feature of many structural choices where economies of large scale are an important feature.

Such decisions are disguised forms of decisions about public goods. Which qualities of water supply out of the large number technically available shall be supplied to the public ? Shall the community possess a set of nuclear weapons and, if so, what types of bomb ? These two sets of question raise in principle the same sort of issues regarding collective decision-making to cope with the externalities that are inevitably associated with all public goods. They raise all the problems which I left unsolved in Chapter III.

# Appendix A

Appendix A

*A Co-ordinated System of Many Controls*

A competitive industry produces $X$ but puts an amount of dirt $D$ into a river which has a flow of clean water $F$, so that $\dfrac{D}{F}$ is the dirt per unit of water. Consumers of water must have water of a certain quality so that the higher is $\dfrac{D}{F}$ the greater is the cost of producing clean water.

There are five ways of coping with the problem of ensuring a proper supply of clean water:

(i)  inducing the industry to produce less $D$;

(ii)  increasing the flow of water $F$;

(iii) getting consumers to filter and clean their own water supply, $W_1$;

(iv) having a public water works to supply clean water, $W_2$; and

(v)  inducing consumers to demand less total clean water,
$$W = W_1 + W_2.$$

In some cases costs will be such that no reliance will be put on one or more of these methods of economising costs. But there is nothing in the nature of things to rule out a solution in which all five methods should be used simultaneously, which would in fact be the case if all methods start with low costs but are subject to rapidly rising costs. The following illustrative exercise is based upon the assumption that such is the case and that all five methods will, therefore, be simultaneously used.

Measure money in units such that the marginal utility of money is unity; and assume that the supply of $X$ and of $W$ makes up a sufficiently small part of the total economy for the marginal utility of money to be unaffected by the measures taken to regulate $X$ and $W$. Then the total contribution of $X$ and $W$ to social utility can be represented as

$$Z = U(X) + U(W_1 + W_2) - A(X,D) - B\left(W_1, \frac{D}{F}\right) - C\left(W_2, \frac{D}{F}\right) - E(F) \quad (1)$$

where $U(X)$ is the utility from the consumption of $X$ and $U(W_1 + W_2)$ the utility from the consumption of $W$. $A(X, D)$ represents the total money cost of production of $X$ and is greater the greater is $X$ and the smaller is $D$, since the abatement of pollution is a costly affair, (i.e. $\dfrac{\partial A}{\partial X} > 0$

and $\dfrac{\partial A}{\partial D} < 0$). $B\left(W_1, \dfrac{D}{F}\right)$ represents the total private cost of production

of an amount of clean water equal to $W_1$ and is the greater, the greater

is the amount of $W_1$ to be produced $\left(\dfrac{\partial B}{\partial W_1} > 0\right)$ and the greater is the

amount of dirt to be extracted from each unit of water $\left(\dfrac{\partial B}{\partial \left(\dfrac{D}{F}\right)} > 0.\right)$

Similarly $C\left(W_2, \dfrac{D}{F}\right)$ is the total cost of the public provision of an amount

of clean water $W_2$ with $\dfrac{\partial C}{\partial W_2}$ and $\dfrac{\partial C}{\partial \left(\dfrac{D}{F}\right)}$ both $> 0$. $E(F)$ is the total cost

to the river authority of ensuring through a system of dams, reservoirs etc.,

a flow of $F$ through the river, with $\dfrac{\partial E}{\partial F} > 0$.

We wish to choose $X$, $W_1$, $W_2$, D and F so as to maximise the expression in (1). The first order conditions for this are:

$$\frac{\partial Z}{\partial X} = U'(X) - \frac{\partial A}{\partial X} = 0 \quad (2)$$

$$\frac{\partial Z}{\partial W_1} = U'(W) - \frac{\partial B}{\partial W_1} = 0 \quad (3)$$

78

$$\frac{\partial Z}{\partial W_2} = U'(W) - \frac{\partial C}{\partial W_2} = 0 \tag{4}$$

$$\frac{\partial Z}{\partial D} = -\frac{1}{F}\left[\frac{\partial B}{\partial\left(\frac{D}{F}\right)} + \frac{\partial C}{\partial\left(\frac{D}{F}\right)}\right] - \frac{\partial A}{\partial D} = 0 \tag{5}$$

$$\frac{\partial Z}{\partial F} = \frac{D}{F^2}\left[\frac{\partial B}{\partial\left(\frac{D}{F}\right)} + \frac{\partial C}{\partial\left(\frac{D}{F}\right)}\right] - \frac{\partial E}{\partial F} = 0 \tag{6}$$

Equation (2) can be written as

$$P_x = \frac{\partial A}{\partial X} \tag{7}$$

since we are assuming that the marginal utility of money is unity. This condition will be satisfied by the competive behaviour of the industry producing $X$.

Equation (3) can similarly be expressed as

$$P_w = \frac{\partial B}{\partial W_1} \tag{8}$$

If the water authority sets a price $P_w$ at which it will supply clean water on demand, then we can assume that private consumers will filter their

own water until the marginal cost of private filtering $\left(\frac{\partial B}{\partial W_1}\right)$ is equal to

the price at which water can be purchased from the water authority ($P_w$).

Equation (4) can be expressed as

$$P_w = \frac{\partial C}{\partial W_2} \tag{9}$$

If the water authority always adjusts its price for clean water until it is

equal to the marginal cost $\left(\frac{\partial C}{\partial W_2}\right)$ of providing the clean water which will

be demanded from it at that price ($P_w$), then this condition will be satisfied.

Suppose the government imposes a tax, $t$, per unit of dirt emitted by the producers of $X$. The profits of the $X$ industry will then be

$P_x X - tD - A(X,D)$.  If the industry is competitive so that each producer takes $P_x$ as given the first order conditions for the maximisation of this profit are

$$P_x = \frac{\partial A}{\partial X}$$

and

$$t = -\frac{\partial A}{\partial D}.$$

The first of these two conditions gives the condition already expressed in equation (7). The second of these two conditions together with equation (5) gives

$$t = -\frac{\partial A}{\partial D} = \frac{1}{F}\left\{ \frac{\partial B}{\partial \left(\frac{D}{F}\right)} + \frac{\partial C}{\partial \left(\frac{D}{F}\right)} \right\} \tag{10}$$

Thus equation (5) will be fulfilled if the government assesses a tax per unit of $D$ equal to $\dfrac{1}{F}$ times the increase in the private and public costs of providing the current amount of clean water which is due to a unit increase in the dirtiness of the river water $\left(\dfrac{D}{F}\right)$.

Equation (6) can then be expressed as

$$\frac{D}{F}t = \frac{\partial E}{\partial F} \tag{11}$$

This condition will be fulfilled if the river authority increases its expenditure on increasing the flow of the river up to the point at which the marginal cost of increasing the flow $F$ is equal to the tax rate on dirt ($t$) multiplied by the dirt per unit of river water $\left(\dfrac{D}{F}\right)$.

Equations 7, 8, 9, 10, and 11 express the proper use of the price-cum-tax mechanism by the consumers and producers of $X$, by the consumers and the private and public producers of clean water $W$, by the water authority, by the governmental taxing authority, and by the river authority.

# Appendix B

*Governmental Regulation of the Structure of Activities*

The purpose of this Appendix is solely to give an idea of the reasons why governmental regulation of the structure of economic activities may be necessary when one activity causes an 'atmospheric' external diseconomy for another economic activity. In order to make the case as sharply as possible a very simple, if unrealistic, model is constructed which displays perfect competition and increasing costs so that, in the absence of externalities, there would be the clearest case for a *laissez-faire* market-mechanism policy.

Assume, therefore, an activity producing electricity ($E$) which it can sell at a given price ($P_E$) in a competitive market. Let its marginal cost of production be $C_E + \gamma_E E$. If a tax at the rate $r$ is imposed on each unit of $E$, then the concern will maximise its profit by equating price to marginal cost plus tax, so that

$$P_E = C_E + \gamma_E E + r$$

*or*  $$E = \frac{M_E - r}{\gamma_E} \qquad (1)$$

Where $M_E = P_E - C_E$

Assume a second industry producing laundry services ($L$) which it can sell at a competitive price $P_L$. Let its marginal cost of production in the absence of smoke from the electricity generating plant be $C_L + \gamma_L L$. But the electricity generating plant produces a given amount of smoke per unit of $E$ produced, and this amount of smoke causes a dirty atmosphere

83

which raises the laundry's cost of producing its laundry services by a given amount per unit of laundry service, regardless of the amount of laundry services produced[1]. Let the cost per unit of laundry services be raised by $\theta E$ where $\theta$ represents the amount of damage done to each unit of laundry service by a unit production of electricity. The laundry will now have a marginal cost of $C_L + \gamma_L L + \theta E$. It will maximise its profit when

$$P_L = C_L + \gamma_L L + \theta E$$

or $\quad L = \dfrac{M_L - \theta E}{\gamma_L}$ \hfill (2)

Where $M_L = P_L - C_L$

Substituting for $E$ from (1) into (2) we have

$$L = \frac{M_L}{\gamma_L} - \theta \frac{M_E - r}{\gamma_E} \frac{}{\gamma_L} \tag{3}$$

Let $L^*$ be the value of $L$ which would rule in the absence of any smoke nuisance and let $E^*$ be the value of $E$ which would rule if it were not taxed, so that

$$L^* = \frac{M_L}{\gamma_L}$$

$$E^* = \frac{M_E}{\gamma_E} \tag{4}$$

Suppose now that both industries are operating in the same locality and that a tax at the rate $r$ is imposed on the output $E$. Figures IV and V illustrate the gain which accrues to society ($G$) from their joint operation. This is equal to the sum of the areas $X + Y + Z$ which is the sum of the values of the outputs ($P_E E + P_L L$) less the cost of the real factors used up in the production of $E$ and $L$. $X$ represents the profits in the electricity industry. $Y$ is the tax revenue received by the central budget. This also represents part of the excess of the value of the electricity generated over the real factor costs involved in its generation, and is thus part of the social surplus, although it accrues to the advantage of the general body

---

[1] This is what is meant by an "atmospheric" externality. The generation of a given output of electricity causes a given pollution of the atmosphere which causes the same amount of dirt per shirt, whether 10 shirts or 1 shirt are hung out to dry.

84

of tax payers rather than to the owners of the electricity works. $Z$ represents the profits in the laundry industry; the rest of its revenue $(P_L L)$ is absorbed by its real factor costs of production, these real costs being swollen by an amount equal to $\theta EL$ because of the need to cope with the dirty atmosphere.

We wish to find the value of $r$ which will maximise the social gain:

$$G = \{X\} + \{Y\} + \{Z\} = \left\{\frac{1}{2}(M_E - r)E\right\} + \left\{rE\right\} + \left\{\frac{1}{2}(M_L - \theta E)L\right\} \quad (5)$$

Substituting for $E$ and $L$ from (1) and (3) and differentiating in respect to $r$ we obtain

$$\frac{dG}{dr} = \frac{1}{\gamma_E}\left\{\theta\left(\frac{M_L}{\gamma_L} - \theta\frac{M_E - r}{\gamma_E}\frac{r}{\gamma_L}\right) - r\right\} = \frac{1}{\gamma_E}(\theta L - r) \quad (6)$$

Differentiating (6) in respect to $r$ we obtain

$$\frac{d^2G}{dr^2} = \frac{1}{\gamma_E}\left(\frac{\theta^2}{\gamma_E\gamma_L} - 1\right) \quad (7)$$

Thus to obtain a maximum for $G$ the first order condition is that $\theta L = r$ and the second order condition is $\theta^2 < \gamma_E\gamma_L$. If $\theta^2 > \gamma_E\gamma_L$, then setting $r = \theta L$ gives a minimum value for $G$.

Let us now consider the variation of the tax $r$ from a value of $r = 0$ to a value of $r = M_E$ at which point (see Figure IV) the production of $E$ ceases to be profitable. Figures VI, VII, VIII, and IX illustrate the six possible cases.

From (6) we can see that, with $r = 0$, $\dfrac{dG}{dr}$ is $\gtrless 0$ according as

$$M_L \gtrless \theta\frac{M_E}{\gamma_E} \quad (8)$$

and that, with $r = M_E$, $\dfrac{dG}{dr}$ is $\gtrless 0$

according as

$$M_E \lessgtr \theta\frac{M_L}{\gamma_L} \quad (9)$$

If $M_L < \theta\dfrac{M_E}{\gamma_E}$ and $M_E < \theta\dfrac{M_L}{\gamma_L}$ then $\theta^2 > \gamma_E\gamma_L$; and conversely if

$M_L > \theta\dfrac{M_E}{\gamma_E}$ and $M_E > \theta\dfrac{M_L}{\gamma_L}$, then $\theta^2 < \gamma_E\gamma_L$.

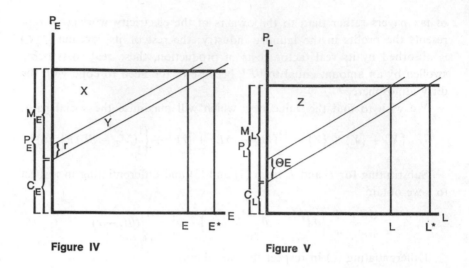

**Figure IV**          **Figure V**

Figure VI represents the case with $M_L > \theta \dfrac{M_E}{\gamma_E}$ (so that at $r = 0$,

$\dfrac{dG}{dr} > 0$) and with $M_E > \theta \dfrac{M_L}{\gamma_L}$ (so that at $r = M_E$, $\dfrac{dG}{dr} < 0$). This is

the stable competitive equilibrium case with both $E$ and $L$ being produced.

Since $M_L > \theta \dfrac{M_E}{\gamma_E}$ and since with $r = 0$, $E = E^* = \dfrac{M_E}{\gamma_E}$, we have $M_L$

$> \theta E^*$, so that even if $E$ were at its maximum level $E^*$ it would still pay
the laundry to operate (see Figure V); and the electricity industry would
operate so long as $r < M_E$ (see Figure IV). Both industries would thus
be profitable and the government by raising $r$ so long as it was less than
$\theta L$ and lowering $r$ so long as it was greater than $\theta L$ would bring the two
industries into the optimum combined level of activities, where $G$ was at a
maximum.

Figure VII represents the case with $M_L < \theta \dfrac{M_E}{\gamma_E}$ (so that at $r = 0$,

$\dfrac{dG}{dr} < 0$) and with $M_E < \theta \dfrac{M_L}{\gamma_L}$ (so that at $r = M_E$, $\dfrac{dG}{dr} > 0$). In this

case we have $\theta^2 > \gamma_E \gamma_L$. In this situation there could be a competitive
equilibrium with both $E$ and $L$ being produced and yet the community

86

would be better off if one or the other activity were forced to close down. The equilibrium would, however, be an unstable one in the sense that θ is so great that, if $r$ were for some reason or another to be raised slightly above its equilibrium level of $r = θL$, the reduction in $E$ would as a result of the high value of θ cause such a large increase in $L$ that we would find $r < θL$. $r$ would then have to be raised further and this process would go on until $r = M_E$ and the $E$-industry would close down entirely leaving the locality solely to the laundry service. Or alternatively if $r$ were lowered slightly below its equilibrium level $r = θL$, the consequential reduction in $E$ would, as a result of a high value of θ, cause so great a reduction in $L$ that $r$ would be found to be greater than θL. $r$ would have to be furthered reduced; and so on, until $L$ was eliminated. For since in this case

$$M_L < θ \frac{M_E}{γ_E} = θE^*, \text{ with } r = 0 \text{ it would be unprofitable to produce any}$$

laundry services.

In this case, therefore, either the $L$-activity or the $E$-activity should close down entirely. But which of these two structures of industry is preferable could not be discovered by the free play of the marginal price-cum-tax mechanism. Some cost-benefit analysis of the total surplus to be obtained in each of the two situations would be necessary. As can be seen from Figures IV and V, the $L$-industry should be the survivor or the victim according as

$$\frac{1}{2}L^* M_L \gtrless \frac{1}{2}E^* M_E$$

$$\text{i.e. as } \frac{M_L^2}{γ_L} \gtrless \frac{M_E^2}{γ_E}$$

Figure VIII shows the case with $M_L > θ \dfrac{M_E}{γ_E}$ and $M_E < θ \dfrac{M_L}{γ_L}$, with

$θ^2 < γ_E γ_L$ in the case of the curvature shown in (a) and $θ^2 > γ_E γ_L$ in

case (b). In these cases both with $r = 0$ and also with $r = M_E$, $\dfrac{dG}{dr} > 0$

(see inequalities (8) and (9)); and since the $G$-curve can change direction only once (see equation (7)), the $G$-curve in these cases must slope consistently upwards from left to right. Moreover, with $\dfrac{dG}{dr}$ consistently $> 0$,

we have $\theta L$ consistently $> r$ (see equation (6)). Since $M_L > \theta \dfrac{M_E}{\gamma_E} = \theta E^*$,

the laundry industry will come into the market even with $r = 0$. Thereafter with $\theta L$ consistently $> r$, the government should raise $r$ until the $E$-activity has been eliminated as it will be at $r = M_E$.

Figure IX shows the cases where $M_L < \theta \dfrac{M_E}{\gamma_E}$ and $M_E > \theta \dfrac{M_L}{\gamma_L}$. In

these cases both with $r = 0$ and also with $r = M_E$, $\dfrac{dG}{dr} < 0$ (see inequalities

(8) and (9)), and the $G$-curve will slope consistently downwards from left

to right. With $r = M_E$, we have $\dfrac{dG}{dr} < 0$ so that the government should

lower $r$. But $r$ remains above $\theta L$ until $r$ is so reduced and $E$ so encouraged that $L$ is knocked out. This will happen before $r$ is reduced to zero be-

cause $M_L < \theta \dfrac{M_E}{\gamma_E} = \theta E^*$, so that $L$-production is unprofitable when $E$ is

at its untaxed level.

Thus in the cases of Figures VI, VIII, and IX the marginal price-cum-tax mechanism will lead to the correct result. But in the case of Figure VII it cannot be relied upon to do so; it may conceivably lead to an equilibrium which will minimise welfare with both $E$ and $L$ in production or, more probably, it may lead to the elimination of $E$ when $L$ should have been the victim or *vice versa*.

Let us confine our attention to the case depicted in Figure VI in which both industries will and should operate together in a competitive equilibrium. This conclusion must however be qualified if there is an alternative location for industry $E$ and/or for industry $L$. Let us suppose that there are two localities which we will call zone A and zone B. Suppose that in zone B the unit cost of $E$ is higher than in zone A by an amount $t_E$ and the unit cost of $L$ is higher in zone B than in zone A by a unit cost $t_L$. We may suppose merely that zone A is the market for $E$ and $L$ and that zone B is

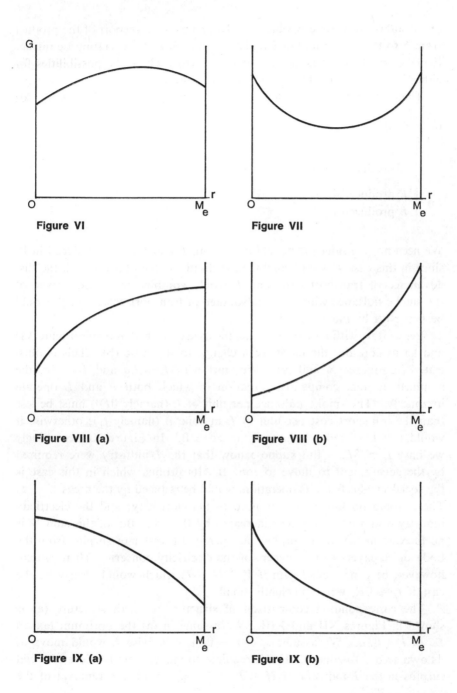

**Figure VI**

**Figure VII**

**Figure VIII (a)**

**Figure VIII (b)**

**Figure IX (a)**

**Figure IX (b)**

89

at a distance from zone A which involves a cost of transport of the product from A to B of $t_E$ per unit of $E$ and $t_L$ per unit of $L$. Let us suppose further that the transport costs are not so high as to exclude the possibilities for either industry of operating at a profit in zone B.

There are now three possible structural arrangements to be considered:

(a)    $E$ and $L$ produced in A

(b) $\left\{ \begin{array}{l} E \text{ produced in A} \\ L \text{ produced in B} \end{array} \right.$

(c) $\left\{ \begin{array}{l} E \text{ produced in B} \\ L \text{ produced in A} \end{array} \right.$

We need not consider the possibility of both $E$ and $L$ being produced in B, since in this case $E$ would combine the disadvantage of a tax with the disadvantage of transport costs and $L$ would combine the disadvantage of the smoke nuisance with the disadvantage of transport costs. Each would be better off by moving to A.

Let us start with structure (a) (i.e. the case described above in Figure VI) and let us consider the merits of a change to structure (b). This is illustrated in Figures X and XI. We start with $E = Ea$ and $L = La$, the assumed optimal competitive situation in which both $E$ and $L$ operate in zone A. The smoke nuisance per unit of $L$ (namely $\theta Ea$) must be less than the transport cost per unit of $L$ in zone B (namely $t_L$); otherwise it would pay $L$ to move voluntarily to zone B. In Figure XI accordingly we have $t_L > \theta Ea$. But suppose now that the $L$-industry were required by the government to move to zone B. Its profits, which in this case is the social surplus from its operation, would be reduced by the areas $U + T$. There would no longer be any need to tax electricity; and the electricity industry would have its profits increased by $W + V$. But of this sum $W$ is no increase in the social surplus, but merely a transfer of surplus from the body of taxpayers to the owners of the electricity concern. There would, however, be a net social gain if $V > U + T$, which would clearly be the case if $t_L - \theta E_a$ were sufficiently small.

The corresponding comparison of structure (c) with structure (a) is shown in Figures XII and XIII. We assume in (a) the optimum tax on $Ea$ of $r = \theta La$. We assume $t_E > r = \theta La$; otherwise $E$ would move of its own accord to zone B. If $E$ is required to move, there is a loss of social surplus in the $E$-industry of $H + J + K + Q$. With the removal of the

90

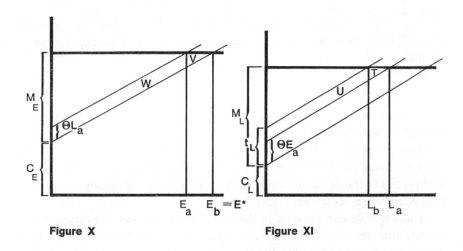

**Figure X**

**Figure XI**

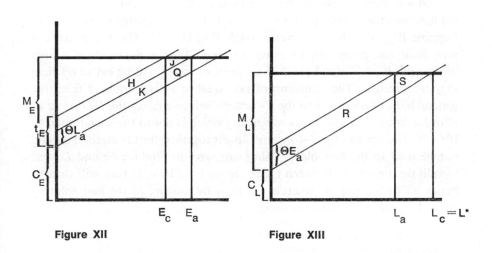

**Figure XII**

**Figure XIII**

smoke nuisance there is a gain of surplus in the laundry industry of $R + S$. But $R = \theta EaLa$ and $K + Q = \theta LaEa$, i.e. both $R$ and $K + Q$ represent an amount equal to the total tax revenue. Thus there is a social gain in moving from (a) to (c) if $S > H + J$, which will be the case if $t_E - \theta L_a$ is sufficiently small.

If $V > U + T$ and at the same time $S > H + J$, then the question arises whether there should be a move to (b) or to (c). This depends upon whether

$$V - (U + T) \gtrless S - (H + J).$$

Thus a movement from (a) to (b) or to (c) may or may not be desirable. In neither case will the marginal price-cum-tax mechanism give rise to such a structural change. Which, if any, structural change is to be promoted must be investigated by some process of social cost-benefit analysis; and if a change is found to be desirable, it must be brought about by some form of governmental structural regulation.

This example can be used to illustrate one other very important point, namely that the tax method of controlling an externality should be used only when it is not possible for the parties concerned to reach a private voluntary agreement to internalise the externality. Suppose that in Figures X, XI, XII, and XIII $V$ is $< U + T$ and $S < H + J$, so that in the social interest structure (a) should be maintained. By a movement from (a) to (b) however, the $L$-industry loses $U + T$ but the $E$-industry gains $W + V$. Suppose $W + V > U + T$, even though $V < U + T$. The $E$-concern can now bribe the $L$-concern to move to zone B by a payment of a sum inbetween $(W + V)$ and $(U + T)$. Both concerns will be better off than they were in (a). The remission of tax equal to $W$ is a transfer from the general body of taxpayers to the $E$-concern, which enables the $E$-concern to afford a bribe to bring about something which is not in the social interest. If the $E$-concern and the $L$-concern can get together, the tax method should not be used in the first place. They can agree to produce $Ea$ and $La$ and to split the amount $W$ between them. Since $V < U + T$, they will then be better off by staying in structure (a) than by moving to (b) and splitting $W + V - (U + T)$ between them.

Achevé d'imprimer
sur les presses de l'Imprimerie Vaudoise
à Lausanne
en septembre mil neuf cent septante-trois